Sam McGredy *and* Seán Jennett

A FAMILY OF ROSES

illustrated by Gillian Kenny

D1728295

Dodd, Mead & Company

First published 1972 in the United States of America
by Dodd, Mead & Company, Inc.

Library of Congress Card Number: 72–38519

I.S.B.N. 0 396 06565 1

Printed in Great Britain by
The Camelot Press Ltd, London and Southampton

For
Niels Poulsen, O.B.N.
of
Denmark

CONTENTS

ILLUSTRATIONS
BY GILLIAN KENNY

*These are some of the fairest rose-children
in the McGredy family—one may call
Poulsen's Pearl an adopted child. They are
reproduced in this book in the chronological
order in which they were introduced to the
public.*

FOREWORD

BY SAM McGREDY

I do not claim to be much of a rose-grower. I know little of spraying procedures, pruning methods, and the like. In fact I must admit that I'm not over fond of gardening, as I have a problem with my back. My ten-acre garden consists of coarse grass and trees. Around my home there is a patio with exactly eight very small rectangular beds smothered with shrubs and ground-cover plants that require absolutely no maintenance. The one exception is a Buddleia and I whack that down to the ground each spring. In the middle of the ten-acre field are ten beds of roses, which I admire but do not personally tend. They contain City of Belfast, Pernille Poulsen, Uncle Walter, Brasilia, Mullard Jubilee, Pania, Irish Mist, Ice White, City of Leeds, and Jan Spek. I thoroughly enjoy watching the trees and shrubs develop their new foliage each spring, and berry in the fall. That is the extent of my gardening interest.

I get a great deal of pleasure from the nursery. But the fine crops we produce are not my work. I am lucky if I get to see them once a month. I became a nurseryman because I was told I had to be a nurseryman. Nobody ever offered me an alternative, and apart from a fleeting desire to be a journalist, no driving ambition pushed me in another direction.

Still, I fell in love with creating roses. On my very first visit to an English flower show, a famous nurseryman told me bluntly that my company's roses were no damned good. That triggered me off, and I set out to prove how wrong he was. On the way I got hooked. Of necessity, I have to breed commercially viable roses, but the real enjoyment is in breeding roses for breeding's sake. I think it would be just the same with cattle or budgerigars or pineapples. It is the simple pleasure of sowing seeds and watching them come up. It is the perfection of a line of seedlings in the field with the morning dew on them. It is the despair of that super yellow hybrid tea covered in mildew. It is the joy of finding a climbing shoot that is going to carry a looked-for second bloom, the agony of a crop failure, the fragrance of apples, mint, and raspberries, the creation, the ability to bend a plant to one's wishes. I did it, it's mine! And it's fun.

And the people who breed roses are fun too. I speak their language and they mine. I would hate all that pleasure to disappear unrecorded and it is for this reason that Seán Jennett and I got together on this book. It is as much a book about people as about roses. The professionalism is Seán's. As we sat and taped our conversations, the ideas and words came out so quickly there was no time to worry about logical order or the Queen's English. As Seán says elsewhere, we are an odd pair, but we work together famously. I think just about our first words to each other were that we never, never would do a book in collaboration with a second person! Amongst the roses, like true Irishmen, we talked a little religion and a lot of politics. Unlike Irishmen, we found we agreed on these subjects. It turned out to be an enjoyable rose 'think-tank'.

I am never completely satisfied with the roses I create and I am dissatisfied in some ways with this book. There wasn't time to write all the things I wanted to say. Each time I read it now I think of other ideas and happenings. I did believe that this kind of book would have more permanence than the average rose book, which dates very quickly. But it isn't true. Already some of my rose-breeding plans are changing as new ideas come to mind. Of one thing I am sure, twenty years from now the rose will be as different from today's model as the Concorde is from the Sopwith Camel. My one ambition in life is to be part of that development.

FOREWORD

BY SEÁN JENNETT

It needs to be said, here at the beginning, to the innocent enthusiast who may expect the usual delightful details about planting, fertilizing, and pruning roses, and other such practical matters, that this book is not a book about rose-gardening. Nevertheless it is a book *for* the rose-gardener, for amateurs of gardens of all sorts, and for those who simply like to theorize in, to look at, and to loaf in other people's gardens—in fact for all those who care to look beyond the beauty of a summer's blossom into that strange ambience from which new roses emerge like so many bright new pennies from a dozen mints. In that sense it is a book about roses, as indeed it should be with such a title and such an author. Sam McGredy is among the most famous, the most eminent of rose-breeders in the world, one of a small, select company whose centres are in various countries of Europe and the U.S.A.—the royal families of roses whose capitals and palaces are glass-houses and their kingdoms rose-nurseries.

In this book Sam McGredy tells discursively, frankly, and often wittily the story of the difficult business of the breeding of new roses and of the commercial drive and acumen that must go with it in order to sell to the public what has been bred. The rose-breeder is an artist, a creator whose creations are often twenty years in the making and seldom less than seven; he therefore has to be an artist of great foresight and immense patience. He achieves his results by blending characteristics and qualities drawn from all over the world and presides over the crucible like an alchemist or a wizard. To these qualities of artist and magician he must

add those of a scientist, and to these, if he is to compete successfully in a highly competitive industry, the abilities of a business-
man. Sam McGredy combines these talents in his own person to
a degree that recalls the versatility of the Renaissance. Yet if he
were called an artist, as he might be, he would be at once flattered,
incredulous, and diffident, and if he were called a tycoon, as he
might be, he would probably reject the description out of hand.

Few men can know more of the work in which they spend
their lives than Sam McGredy does of his, and his knowledge is
not confined or local, but global. He is perpetually in motion
from his centre in Northern Ireland over the whole world, and
there is scarcely a rose-breeder or a rose-propagator of any
importance whose work is unknown to him. No one could be
better qualified by experience to write this book.

My part has been a minor one. I have written the first two
chapters as an introduction to the rest, as an outsider venturing to
lead outsiders. Beyond those chapters my principal function has
been to serve as editor. The book is based on a series of long
conversations between Sam and myself at his house at Mullavilly,
conversations that were tape-recorded as we spoke. Some details
come from meetings in London. 'Conversations', I have said,
but in fact they were really a series of *ad hoc* lectures delivered by
Sam with such charm, clarity, and enthusiasm that I could not
fail to have been deeply imbued with similar colour. The taped
notes made about two hundred pages of typed quarto sheets,
to which I added some scores more from a study of the press-
cuttings of the McGredy business from 1914 to the present time,
and from talks I had with Sam's mother Mrs. Ruth McGredy and
with his uncle Mr. Walter Johnston.

Noticeable in these press-cuttings are frequent references to
the charm of the successive heads of the McGredy nursery; after
Sam IV took over the direction of the business such references
became more numerous. As most of the writers were Englishmen,
the charm, of course, is always 'Irish charm', an ineffable quality
that appears to the English mind as something to which all
Irishmen are born, as though they imbibed it from the soft Irish

air, floated in it in the natal fluid of their mother's womb, or at their birth were suspended in some thick sweet syrup as Achilles was dipped by his mother in the Styx. It is all boloney (which looks like a good Irish word—but is Italian). Irishmen sometimes have a quiet satirical chuckle at the illusions of the English concerning the Irish.

There, perhaps, is a light to lead us. Americans are sometimes amazed, though enchanted, to find that most Englishmen say 'please' and 'thank you' as a matter of custom. American society has largely dispensed with such antique courtesies. England, quaint England, is behind the American times, but it is on the way to catch up. Ireland is still farther back, and its good manners, firmly based on a sincere desire to please the visitor and to be friendly, are more apparent. That is what 'Irish charm' really is.

Sam McGredy has something more. I have never met anyone whom I have so quickly come to like and to respect, so quickly come to regard as a friend. I, it should be said, am an introvert and not the most forthcoming of people, but my heart goes out to Sam McGredy. Sam, you might suppose on first acquaintance, is an extrovert; he is nothing of the sort—he is a deeply sensitive person of instinctive taste and open friendliness.

The house on the hill that is the home of Sam and his wife Maureen and their two daughters is an unusual building. Designed by Adair Roche and built in 1967, it is principally a single storey from the centre of which rises a three-storey tower with a canted roof. All three bedrooms, three bathrooms, a sauna bath, a bar, and the living-rooms are on the ground floor, in a kind of serpentine open plan in which the only doors lead to the bedrooms and the bathrooms. The first floor of the tower was designed as Maureen's sitting-room; as it contains a colour-television set, the room becomes, when they are home from school, the domain of the children. Above, on the top floor, is Sam's study, with a wide window looking southwards over the undulating fields of the rose-nursery and over an old linen-mill half-sunk in a valley, which is the nursery's packing-station. The fields change from year to year in a four-year rotation, so that sometimes a tide of roses laps up to the boundaries of the garden and sometimes cattle roam where the roses were and will be again. There are few buildings—a former farmhouse that is to be the new nursery office, the mill, and the small, grey, Victorian church of Mullavilly with a tower bravely trying to dominate the fields. The view is southwards towards the Irish Republic, which is glimpsed, when the weather is clear, as a distant heave of hills. Around the nursery, hidden among the folds of the land, are dozens of town-lands, hamlets, and villages, and a few towns such as Tandragee and, farther off, Portadown, where the McGredy nursery was founded. A 'townland' in Ireland is no more than a part of a parish; it may not have a single house on it, but it will have a name. Almost every place-name is Gaelic, its spelling mishandled by the English as they mishandle the spellings of so many other languages, including their own. 'Mullavilly' itself (a townland) is Gaelic, meaning a 'bare hill'; 'Tandragee' is Gaelic and so too is 'Portadown', and most place-names in the north and through-out Ireland, even 'Belfast'. In these names ancient Ireland from the iron age to the middle ages surges still around the modern nursery and the house on the bare hill of Mullavilly.

PART
ONE

1. THE McGREDY FAMILY

There have been four Samuel McGredys in the nursery business in Northern Ireland. The list begins with Samuel McGredy I, who was born in 1828 and died in 1903. He was head gardener of one of those large estates that are called 'demesnes' in Ireland, most of which have long since been divided into smaller holdings. At the age of about fifty he left this employment to strike out on his own. He leased ten acres of land just outside Portadown, with a small greenhouse, and there he started growing pansies as a business—there seems to be no evidence that the founder of the McGredy fortunes took any special interest in roses, though at that time the hybrid perpetuals were in vogue and the hybrid tea roses were soon to begin their long hold upon the market. Breeding roses was then, as at all times, a costly affair and it is probable that the first Sam McGredy in the nursery business had to conserve a modest capital and to use it in a way that would give him a quicker turnover than the growing of roses was likely to do. The little greenhouse survived until very recently, and the ten acres, added to from time to time, remains the nucleus of the nursery. The land is now zoned as part of the new city of Craigavon and plans are afoot to move to the new land near Tandragee. The twenty-roomed house next to the cottage, which became the home of the family for fifty or sixty years, has been transformed into the Craigavon Inn, a superior kind of pub with a very good restaurant, founded by Samuel McGredy IV and his friends David Magill and Michael Donaghy. The rose-breeding and propagating business has now been transferred to a complex of undulating fields south of Portadown, covering more than 210 acres.

The second Sam McGredy was born in 1861, and he was therefore about nineteen years old when his father decided to begin on his own account. It was perhaps Sam II who introduced the breeding of roses into the business some time in the late 1890s, for he was exhibiting in 1905, two years after his father's death, and it is generally agreed that he could not have bred a winning rose in these first two years of his sole control. His first success was to win a gold medal at the National Rose Society show for a hybrid tea, the Countess of Gosford. It was very much the fashion in those days to name roses after people, either relatives, friends, or patrons. There followed a series of roses that gained gold medals at the National Rose Society's shows. These included Iris Stanley in 1909, Mrs. Herbert Stevens in 1910, Edward Mawley in 1911, Mrs. Charles E. Pearson in 1913, Leona Herdman in 1914, and Miss Willmott in 1917. Also in 1917 the firm introduced Golden Emblem, a good yellow rose derived from the Pernetiana series developed by Pernet-Ducher. A year later the trade was excited by the appearance from Portadown of a fine new rose, The Queen Alexandra Rose, with petals of bright vermilion and old gold. This rose was extensively used in the McGredy nurseries for breeding, its progeny including the orange-scarlet Margaret McGredy and the scarlet-copper-orange Mrs. Sam McGredy.

After the first world war Samuel McGredy II developed and exhibited a series of fine roses. Among them was one of the most enduring and attractive of roses, called Mrs. Charles Lamplough, which was used for breeding as late as 1958, and also Mabel Morse, a hybrid tea described in 1923 by Courtney Page, editor of the National Rose Society annual, as far and away the best of the yellow hybrid teas.

Sam II died in 1926, and a year later the Margaret McGredy rose appeared, named after his wife, the first rose to bear the name McGredy.

Sam McGredy III was twenty-nine when his father died. The firm was already in the forefront of rose-breeding and of the rose market, and Sam III now set out to undertake the breeding of roses more scientifically and on a larger scale. The result was what his son, Sam IV, has described as the golden years of the rose business in Portadown. They may be said to have begun with one of the best roses of this century, Mrs. Sam McGredy, which has petals of a copper-orange flushed with red on the outside. This hybrid tea rose appeared in 1929 and is still to be found in many catalogues together with a climbing version. Forty years is a long life for a modern rose, long not only in the sense that it has held its favour with rose gardeners, but also in that it has retained its vigour so well. It was followed by McGredy's Ivory and then in 1932 by Picture, a deep pink, and in 1933 by McGredy's Yellow, bred from The Queen Alexandra Rose.

But then abrupt disaster came upon the firm of Samuel McGredy & Son. Sam McGredy III died suddenly, in 1934, of a heart attack. The firm was left leaderless, the present Sam McGredy, that is the fourth, being at that time a child of two years. A board of four trustees was formed to look after the running of the nurseries and the family affairs. This board included Mrs. Ruth McGredy, wife of Sam III, and her brother-in-law Walter Johnston. A rose-nursery business is a highly personal one, and its owner or manager cannot very well be a faceless man. In Walter Johnston, the McGredys were highly fortunate, for Walter, 'Uncle Walter', threw himself into the business with all his heart and kept it going successfully until the war came along. Rose-nurseries were clearly not essential to the war effort, and the fields then had to be sown to food crops of various kinds, the packing-sheds grew mushrooms, and the greenhouses became prolific producers of tomatoes. Walter Johnston found himself directing a large market-garden. What could be saved of the breeding-stock of roses was pushed up into one corner, where they could be preserved to recommence rose-breeding when the war ended and better times came again.

The early post-war years were not highly productive of prize-winning roses; it takes time to bring a nursery back on course. In 1948 the red Rubaiyat won the All-America Award, a success that brought it on to the rich American market. The following year the curious rose called Grey Pearl, a kind of dull lavender, startled everybody. The first of the race of lavender-blue roses, it was known as the Mouse among the nursery staff.

Meanwhile Sam McGredy IV was growing up. As his father and his grandfather, he grew into a tall man, some 6ft. 3in. in height, and with the burliness to match, so that he looks like, what indeed at college he was, a hefty rugby player. There seems to be something in this business of rose-growing that makes for tallness, for several other rose-breeders are as tall as Sam McGredy, or taller, making an exception, the diminutive Jan Spek of Holland, look very small when he is in this company—as he often is, the members of the rose-growing fraternity being indeed fraternal and in the habit of making frequent visits to each other.

Sam IV went to Mercersburg Academy, Pennsylvania, for a time as an exchange student, and then took horticultural courses at Greenmount College and Reading University, with what he calls conspicuous lack of success. This was followed by a year at Slocock's nursery at Woking, in Surrey, to gain experience of the nursery business in general.

Sam McGredy IV, born in 1932, was twenty when, back in Ireland, his Uncle Walter handed him the keys of the breeding-house and told him it was all his. Uncle Walter, who had himself been pitched unexpectedly into rose-breeding and propagating, probably thought that a similarly abrupt initiation was the best thing for young Sam. And so in fact it was. In gratitude for his work in the nursery Sam named a rose Uncle Walter (*facing page* 44); it is a rich red, the winner of two gold medals.

Young Sam had no special knowledge of rose-breeding or of rose-propagation, and no experience of the actual business of pollinating and budding, as most other rose-breeders have. Nor, he determined, was he going to spend time on learning how to do these operations. There was no need. There was a well trained and competent staff who would pollinate roses and raise seedlings under his direction. It was Sam, however, who chose the pairs of roses to breed from, Sam who selected the seedlings that seemed best to suit his aims and directed them to be budded to understocks

Poulsens Pearl

and planted out in the fields; and it was Sam who walked the long rows of maiden plants looking for their best qualities and choosing those that were to be used in continuing work for new varieties. He has, no doubt, a closer identification with the roots of his business than, let us say, an industrialist has with the operations on the factory floor, but he keeps away from time-consuming manual work in order to pursue his business aims. It is amusing in this context to note that a number of McGredy customers interviewed by a market-investigation firm considered that Sam's image in the rose-business was disappointing because he habitually appeared in a business suit rather than in rough old garden clothes.

His father, Sam III, had brought order and a certain science into the business of breeding roses, and Sam IV pursued this policy, maintaining careful records and charts by means of which the crossings of many roses through several generations can be traced, together with information concerning the results. He has been successful in breeding many fine new roses that have enhanced the reputation of the McGredy nurseries throughout the world. He has followed that reputation and supported it by frequent visits to shows and to breeders, propagators, and customers in many countries; he is still likely to hop on a plane at a moment's notice to descend on an important nursery in Birmingham, England, in Portland, Oregon, or in Paris, or in Tokyo. He certainly travels more than most businessmen do. The scale and quality of the business may be gauged from the fact that he sells a million rose plants every year and his firm is generally recognized as one of the best breeders of garden roses in the world.

In 1959 Sam McGredy became engaged to Maureen McCall, a tall, dark-haired Irish girl following a career as a fashion model. Sam declared that she should be a queen of roses and that one day he would name a rose after her, as other roses had been named for women of the McGredy family; but it should be one of the finest roses, and no such rose existed at that time in his nursery. Nor has it appeared yet—Sam's standard is high. He might, of course, ask Maureen to choose, as his mother was asked, a rose for herself. Mrs. Sam McGredy, wife of Sam III, invited to select from a collection of the best the nursery could offer a rose to bear her name, rejected them all and picked an unconsidered rose from those that had been left out as not good enough. Her rejected rose became, as it proved, one of the best-selling and longest-enduring of roses in garden catalogues, where you may find it still to this day.

There are two daughters of the marriage, Kathryn and Maria. The question is obvious—whether a woman could run the nursery as well as any of the four Sams. She would need to have the energy and endurance to cope with the international ramifications of the business as well as an eye for the qualities of a rose. The girls are still children and the answer is far in the future. Sam says that he is socialist enough to believe it more important that roses should continue to be grown in Portadown than that a McGredy should do it.

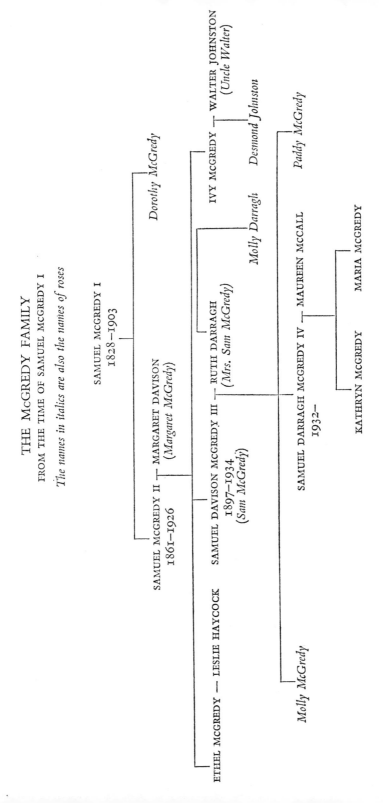

THE McGREDY FAMILY

FROM THE TIME OF SAMUEL McGREDY I

The names in italics are also the names of roses

SAMUEL McGREDY I
1828–1903

SAMUEL McGREDY II
1861–1926

MARGARET DAVISON
(*Margaret McGredy*)

Dorothy McGredy

IVY McGREDY — WALTER JOHNSTON
(*Uncle Walter*)

Desmond Johnston

Molly Darragh

SAMUEL DAVISON McGREDY III
1897–1934
(*Sam McGredy*)

RUTH DARRAGH
(*Mrs. Sam McGredy*)

ETHEL McGREDY — LESLIE HAYCOCK

SAMUEL DARRAGH McGREDY IV — MAUREEN McCALL
1932–

Paddy McGredy

Molly McGredy

KATHRYN McGREDY

MARIA McGREDY

2. THE TECHNIQUE OF ROSE-BREEDING

All cultivated roses are descended from one wild rose or another, or, as is more probable, from a number of wild roses the strains of which have been crossed and tangled by interbreeding throughout a thousand years. The result of all this crossing of strains is that, though wild roses may come true from seed, cultivated roses seldom do. Instead, cultivated roses give rise, by seed, to a surprising variety of seedlings that do not appear to conform to the Mendelian principles of heredity. They would be seen to conform if we could project Mendel's principles through a thousand generations with full knowledge of what the origins of the roses were and of the species and varieties that had been introduced into the line.

Cultivated roses, therefore, cannot be propagated for the market by seed; but a new variety does begin with seed—with seed produced by fertilizing a selected rose with pollen from another rose. Roses are bisexual—that is, they comprise male and female organs in one flower. The male organs are the anthers, the pollen-bearing capsules standing on the ends of slender filaments in the centre of the rose. The female organ is the stigma, the yellow, button-like central boss of the flower. Self-fertilization may occur by pollen falling from the anthers on to the stigma. Cross-fertilization from another flower or another plant occurs through the medium of bees or flies carrying pollen grains from one flower to another. Beneath the rose is the receptacle, which in time becomes the familiar hip. It contains the seeds or ovules, which are connected by tubular structures to the stigma. When a ripe pollen grain falls upon the slightly tacky stigma it is held there. The grain puts out a long tube, which enters the stigma and makes its way down to one of the ovules, which it fertilizes. The petals of the rose will now begin to fade and die away and the hip changes colour while the seeds within it develop and harden into carpels.

In a rose-breeding nursery pollination is done by human hand. The pollen from one rose is used to fertilize another rose, both selected by the rose-breeder because they appear to carry characteristics that he hopes they will transmit to their progeny. The growing of breeding-plants and the operation of pollination take place in a greenhouse, where the climate can be controlled and from which insects may be excluded—if any insects do get in they are soon killed by vaporizing insecticides. The breeder carefully cuts the anthers from the two roses he intends to cross; this must be done when the flowers are about half-open and before the anthers are quite ripe and ready to shed their pollen. The anthers are then laid on named or numbered sheets of paper to ripen in the warmth of the air. In Sam McGredy's breeding-house the anthers are laid on their papers on a trolley, which runs on rails down the central aisle and allows the work to be done with considerable economy of labour.

When the anthers are ripe they will open and shed their pollen. Many breeders use a small water-colour brush to pick up some of the pollen grains and apply them to the stigma of the rose to be fertilized. This method requires the brush to be sterilized after each use. Sam McGredy prefers to use a finger for pollinating because a finger can be quickly licked clean ready for the next rose. Many breeders strip their pollinated roses of all their petals, but Sam leaves a ring of petals intact, because after fertilization these petals quickly begin to fade and he can, by merely glancing at them, determine whether a rose has or has not been successfully pollinated. The pollinated roses, of course, are labelled as they are dealt with. A chart is kept, too, to show at a glance which roses have been pollinated and what kind of pollen has been used for each.

In due course the receptacle below each pollinated rose will develop into a hip with the hard seeds or 'carpels' within it. This takes several months, into the autumn. The hips are then picked from the plant, each with its label, and they are buried upside down in warm, damp peat or vermiculite in order to mature the seed and rot away or soften the wall of the hip and so allow the seeds to be easily extracted. The seeds are then washed in water; those that float are probably infertile and can be thrown away.

The next stage is to sow the seeds in shallow soil on benches in a greenhouse. In a normal season Sam McGredy may have as many as 150,000 seedlings growing from seeds of roses pollinated in the manner described, each seedling producing blooms; these blooms are smaller in the first year than they would eventually be, but they are sufficient to indicate colour and quality. Day by day, as they come into blossom, Sam examines the plants and sticks a cane into the soil beside each one he wishes to carry further in his breeding programme. He cannot, however, at this stage say definitely that any rose is going to be a good new variety, for roses do not always bloom in their first year as they will when fully established. He must choose by experience and often by playing a hunch.

He may mark with his canes as many as three thousand seedlings. These seedlings are used to supply buds for the next operation, the budding of understocks in the field. Five understocks are budded from each selected seedling, so he now has fifteen thousand roses from one year's cross-pollination growing in his fields. The buds are cut from the parent seedling with a small piece of stem attached, and each bud is inserted into a T-shaped cut in the base of the stem of its understock, where it is secured by means of a rubber tie; raffia was formerly used to tie the bud on, but rubber is much quicker. The understocks used at Portadown are *Rosa multiflora*. After the buds have taken on the understock, that is during the winter, the upper part of the understock plant is cut off and burnt.

The budded roses do not flower until the following summer. As they come into bloom, Sam McGredy and his right-hand man, Harry McKeown, tramp daily along the rows—a total

Mischief

distance of several miles, and in the height of the flowering season they do it twice a day—to see what his lottery aided by foresight and hunch is bringing him in the way of new roses. Vigour and disease-resistance, colour and form of the bud and of the flower, colour and character of the foliage, the habit of the plant, and perfume, if any, are the characteristics that are considered. A few plants, only a fraction of the original number, are selected for further trials, and possibly as breeding-roses for a new generation. Eventually there may be a few dozen roses out of the thousands budded that are worth further work, and these are grown to provide buds for plants for the trials of the Royal National Rose Society at St. Albans. Plants also go to other trial-grounds throughout the world, where they will be subjected to climates very different from those in which they were grown at Portadown in Ulster. Groups of four are also sent to the members of the Better Roses Club founded by Sam McGredy IV for amateurs who would like to take part in the development of new roses. As the roses grow in these trial-grounds they are carefully judged and are awarded points for various characteristics. This 'pointing' provides a valuable guide to the qualities of a rose and to its probable popularity on the market.

A rose that has come successfully through all its trials and tests is introduced to the public through the medium of rose-shows, though it has to be said that rose-shows are in general neither as numerous nor as important as they once were. The awards gained, however, are still valued by some and quoted with pride in sales literature and catalogues.

It will be seen from this account of the genesis of a new rose that every plant of that variety put on the market is directly derived from the stem of the first seedling of its kind. This is asexual or vegetative propagation, and it is necessary to ensure that all the plants of the variety come true to form and description. Such a group is called a 'clone' or 'clon', from a Greek word meaning a twig or slip. In the case of such a rose as Peace, by Meilland, one of the most popular roses ever bred, the clone of millions of plants throughout the world represents millions of buds taken from the original plant or from other plants that have been budded from the original one. In time a deterioration sets in, and the variety has to be withdrawn from the market. That period is not by any means the same for each rose. The rose Mrs. Sam McGredy has been going strong for forty years, Peace itself is still vigorous after more than thirty years, and some roses, such as Madame Caroline Testout, raised by Pernet-Ducher in 1890, have been on the market for eighty years or more. Many modern varieties, more interbred and more distant from the wild species, keep their vigour for a much shorter time, and an examination of catalogues of ten years ago will show many once-popular varieties that are no longer obtainable. This deterioration, of course, does not mean that any of these short-lived varieties established in private gardens are suddenly going to fall flat at the expiration of the term, or necessarily for many years afterwards. Roses of any variety, when properly tended, are long-lived plants. In compensation for the shorter life, modern roses produce better-formed and larger and more abundant blooms than do most older roses with longer lives.

The breeding of roses and the winning of awards for roses is only the first part of the business of a rose-nursery. The second part is the propagating of plants to obtain sufficient quantities to meet the expected demand when the rose is at last placed on the market. In this as in any other business the breeder must estimate how many of his product he will be able to sell and must match the scale of production to meet that figure. A large part of the nursery is therefore given up to growing roses for the market. The process begins with the planting of understocks in the fields, and continues with the raising of sufficient plants of the new variety to provide the quantity of buds for grafting on to the understocks, to be ready for sale at the optimum time of the rose-gardener's year.

Not all rose-growers are breeders of roses. There are many firms selling roses mainly as propagators—one of the best-known is Harry Wheatcroft & Sons of Edwalton, Nottingham, a firm well known to rose-gardeners and to television viewers by the handle-bar moustache of its founder. These propagating firms obtain plants or buds from the breeders and, under licence, bud from these to build up stocks for sale.

In addition, there is an interlocking mesh of agencies by which rose-breeders and rose-propagators of one country act as agents for rose-breeders in other countries, propagating each other's roses in their nurseries for sale on their home market. Sam McGredy, for example, is agent in the British Isles for roses bred by Kordes of Germany, and by Poulsen of Denmark; he propagates plants from these firms and buds from them to raise quantities for sale. This is a common practice throughout the rose trade. The plants should always be identified by the name of the breeder, but this is frequently neglected.

Trials and awards

Roses planted out in the many trial-grounds throughout the world help to demonstrate the qualities—and faults—of a new variety. They show how resistant it may be to the diseases that sometimes afflict roses and how well it stands up to different kinds of climate and weather. These matters are taken into account in any pointing or awards that may be given. Among the most important trials and awards in the British Isles are those of the Royal National Rose Society, whose trial-grounds are at St. Albans. A panel of twenty judges examines the roses there at intervals throughout the season from June to September over two or three successive years.

Trial-Grounds Certificates are issued by the society to roses that have been grown for at least two years in the trial-grounds and that have been proved true to type and suitable for ordinary cultivation.

Certificates of Merit are awarded after three years in the trial-grounds to roses of special quality. Exceptionally, very fine roses may be given a Certificate of Merit after only two years.

The Society's Gold Medal is awarded to very few roses and only to those of quite exceptional quality. Only two or three medals

23

are awarded each year; in some years, when no worthy contender is found, no medal is awarded.

The President's International Trophy is awarded to the gold-medal winner that is considered worthy of the highest honour the society can bestow. In some years, as in 1962 and 1966, no rose is considered sufficiently good and no award of the trophy is made.

The Henry Edland Memorial Medal, instituted in 1966, is awarded annually to the most fragrant seedling of the year, which must not be lower in quality than the standard of the Certificate of Merit. This medal has replaced the Clay Cup—a similar award to British roses made before 1966.

Other trials and awards

Belfast has a beautiful trial-ground founded at the instigation of Sam McGredy IV and Craig Wallace, secretary of the Rose Society of Northern Ireland. It differs from other trial-grounds in requiring not six plants but twenty-five, and the effect of a mass of blooms of one variety may thus be better appreciated. The supreme prizes are the Golden Thorn, a large and fearsome rose thorn of gold and metal for the best floribunda, and the City of Belfast Gold Medal for the best hybrid tea.

The All-America Rose Selection Organization is a society of commercial rose-growers who run trials of roses in twenty-two trial-grounds spread across the United States from the East Coast to Oregon and down to California, with a wide variety of climatic conditions. The judges' results are considered by a committee of nurserymen and a majority must be in favour of any rose selected for an award. An All-America Award is important to the commercial success of a rose in the U.S.A.

Other trials and awards take place in various Continental countries—in Scandinavia, in Germany, in Rome, in Geneva, in Holland, in Madrid, and in the garden of the eighteenth-century Château de Bagatelle in the Bois de Boulogne in France; Michelin describes the rose garden at Bagatelle as an *éblouisse-ment*.

Evelyn Fison

Rose-shows

All flower-shows have classes for roses and for long it was important for rose-breeders and propagators to have stands and displays in nearly every show. The most important shows in these islands are the one at Southport and the Chelsea Flower Show. Shows were until recently the most popular means by which the public might see both new and established roses. The four McGredys spent a great deal of time attending shows and building up elaborate displays of thousands of plants and cut-blooms. Sam II and Sam III had to dispatch their roses to shows by train and steamer, and there were occasions when the consignments went astray, so that when they did at last arrive Sam II or Sam III had to work throughout the night arranging the exhibit. On another occasion, at Chelsea, work was still going on as the visitors streamed in. Sam IV used air transport, booking several seats on passenger planes so that the roses could be carried in three boxes to a seat. This was expensive and later it was found cheaper to charter a Dakota especially to carry the roses.

Strange things sometimes happened at shows. Once Sam had part of his exhibit stolen, and another time a whole flowering rose-bush disappeared without any of scores of eyes perceiving its passing. Sam IV on one occasion found a large but very live duck lying beneath one of his bowls of roses and at Southport in 1962 a white rabbit was discovered contentedly munching the leaves and flowers of Sam's exhibit. Practical jokers abound in the trade.

Shows such as these were important in the sales of roses, and customers could come up to a stand and place their order on the spot. The advantages of shows to sales has declined with the advent of garden-centres, where in effect there are rose-shows and flower-shows throughout the season, with all the plants waiting to be bought. The garden-centres have also had an effect on the mail-order business, which declined severely in the sixties. Sam McGredy IV has opened a flourishing garden-centre at Derriaghy, near Belfast, where customers may see many thousands of roses and other plants, and he is planning to franchise others.

Patents for roses

One of the most difficult aspects of the rose business, and one that caused heart-burning for many years, was the lack of protection in law of new roses. A breeder producing a new rose over a period of several years and expending large sums of money in the process had no means of protecting his investment. It was open to anyone to buy a plant or two of any variety, new or established, as the foundation of a propagating programme that within a few months could produce thousands of plants of that variety, which could be put on the market in competition with those of the breeder and at a lower price. The propagator not having had to lay out any capital in breeding the variety was in fact taking advantage of the breeder's investment to compete unfairly against him. All that the original breeder could do was to work at top speed to get the variety on to the market before anyone else and hope to recoup some of his capital outlay by his sales during a month or two, or at the most a season, before any competitor caught up.

There was a good deal of agitation in the early fifties concerning the need for a new law or regulation that would secure to the breeder the rights in his product, in the same manner as the patent right of a new invention or the copyright of a new book. The trouble was made worse by the advent of reciprocal rose patents in other countries. French and German breeders, for example, each enjoyed protection in their own country and in the others', but English roses could be legally pirated in either country for lack of a rose patent and reciprocal agreement.

In 1955 Sam McGredy wrote to Major Gwillym Lloyd George, Minister of Agriculture, who had made a visit to Northern Ireland, as follows:

'First of all you will appreciate that a new rose is raised from seed. Once the variety is obtained, it is propagated purely by budding or grafting on to a wild-rose stock. When we put the pollen of one rose on to the stigma or female organ of another, the chance of obtaining a commercial variety by sowing the seed is very slender. In fact, we must raise many thousands of seedlings to obtain one worthwhile variety. The expense incurred is in the region of £2,000 per rose.

'Once we offer this rose on the British market, we lose control of it within six months, as anybody is entitled to grow it without paying the raiser a royalty. As a result plant-breeding and research in horticulture is not a paying proposition in Great Britain. On the other hand, France, Belgium, Holland, Scandinavia, Germany, and the U.S.A. have plant protection for their hybridists. This protection has encouraged them to improve their research stations and consequently practically 100 per cent of the best new rose varieties are raised abroad and eventually find their way on to the British market. Not only does this affect our sales at home but our export trade is dropping alarmingly due to the competition stimulated by the patents acts in these countries. In fact, we have not, for example, exported one new rose variety to the U.S.A. since 1947. We simply cannot afford to raise large quantities of seedlings to obtain one or two worthwhile novelties unless we are afforded some protection and stimulant in Great Britain. . . .

'It is not our intention to try and create a monopoly with any new roses created in the future. In fact, it is obvious that it would be to our advantage to license any British nurseryman wishing to grow these varieties, on payment of a small royalty, as is done all over the rest of the world.

'Briefly, our argument is this: a plant patent will allow us to command a small royalty from the British rose-growers. It will also enable us to extend our research department enabling us to compete with foreign hybridists.'

This letter was well received and had an effect, but government being as ponderous as it is, it was some years before an Act giving protection to plant-breeders was presented to Parliament. In the meantime, powerful opposition came into being, led by propagators, who would have preferred to go on as they were. The aim of this opposition, if it could not prevent the Act from becoming law, was to reduce the royalty to a percentage too small to have much effect. This opposition was unsuccessful and the Bill became law in 1964.

PART
TWO

3. ROSE-BREEDING

I do not think that one can always say when the breeding of a new rose begins. Breeding is a continuous process requiring knowledge and experience and capital, and somewhere in the stream a new rose begins to show, perhaps first merely as an idea, a perception, which I pursue and try to develop. A breeder has, I think, to know what has gone before. My bible is a reference book called *Modern Roses 7*—'7', that is, because that is the latest edition, *Modern Roses* 1 to 6 having come out earlier.* *Modern Roses 7* lists every rose that has been put on the market, and gives its breeder and its parentage. I read this book from cover to cover and then read it again and again. In addition I have the breeding records of the McGredy roses for study—but they are not complete; a gap from 1918 to 1925 was caused by an over-zealous girl having a scrap-drive during the war. My father died when I was between two and three and so I have no direct connection with what he did and what his experience was. When I came into the McGredy business I had to start from scratch.

It was no good emulating what other people were doing, for following someone else's strain is a waste of time. I had to build my own, so I read the best books and I took the best roses from almost every nursery, that is from the best breeders of the time, Boerner's best, and the best of the old McGredy roses, bred by my father and my grandfather, and all the other greats, and I gathered them all together in a greenhouse. Then I wafted pollen about from one to another without any real regard for what I was doing and what would come of it. I just wanted to see what would happen. And I got nothing. Nothing!

* *Modern Roses 7*, J. Harris McFarland of Harrisburg, Pa.

That was my first year. I bred a lot of roses and found that nearly all of the product and its making was a waste of time. Only three or four plants seemed at all worth keeping. I went on from there, learning that such and such a rose—Karl Herbst is an example—will often give roses with black marks on the outer petals, will nearly always give a full flower, and will give a plant of awkward habit, while Spartan will usually produce progeny with small flowers of good form and fragrance. I found also that it is usually possible by breeding to change the colour from yellow to dark crimson. You learn these things by observation and by trial and error, and that is the way to start, or at least the way I started.

Rose-breeding is a continuous planning process, and at the beginning of every year I make a study of the results of my crosses from the previous year. I do a statistical extract first of all to see what percentage of crosses are promising. It is always helpful to know, for instance, that Fragrant Cloud is throwing a high percentage of good-looking seedlings, and that it is clearly worth going on with that rose and that line. Then I look again to see which parent roses are producing good characteristics, the characteristics that I am looking for. I go from there and decide which plants I want to throw out of the breeding-house and which I want to bring in. Then I sit down with my breeding-charts, which show down the left-hand side all the hips I have used and along the top all the pollens that I have available, plus other pollens that I want to introduce. I cross-check them and mark them down by blocking out the squares where the appropriate pollen and flower meet at the intersections of the vertical and lateral lines on the chart.

I don't plan for a specific rose—unless, that is, I think I am on the way to a super-red hybrid tea, and everybody is looking for that. I plan, otherwise, for half a dozen up to perhaps twenty different things, but, like every other hybridist at this point of time, if I saw a super-red hybrid tea coming out I would pursue it diligently. Kordes has raised a line of hybrid teas, the best of which, I think, is Ernest E. Morse. Tantau has raised a string of them, but none of them of first importance. Armstrong's in the U.S.A., nothing at all; Herb Swim's Oklahoma and Mr. Lincoln are acceptable but not *very* good in this part of the world, although they are near the top in America. What we are all looking for is a crimson to crimson-scarlet. Dickson has raised Red Devil, which is blue-red, and the blue in it is the fault. He has also raised Red Planet, which is very good. Alec Cocker has bred Alec's Red, another good red rose, while my contribution has been John Waterer and National Trust, both good, but with faults. National Trust bears a bloom of beautiful shape, beautiful in everything, but it has no fragrance. John Waterer has a fantastic flower and abundant fragrance, but in heavy rain it hangs its head. What I would like to see is a Papa Meilland without the faults of that rose—it gets lots of mildew and does not weather well, and the plant is really not very fine, but the colour is a deep, deep red, and that is what I would like to get, on plants that are reasonably disease-free and healthy and vigorous with blooms that will withstand the rains. In the summer conditions of the south of France, where it was bred, Papa Meilland is a magnificent rose.

I would also like to raise yellow floribundas that do not fade. In the next ten years there are, I think, going to be a number of roses of orange colours. I am trying to raise these both in floribundas and in hybrid teas. And I am also trying to follow up what I call my 'hand-painted' roses, such as Picasso (*facing page* 136), in these other colours.

One of my problems is to imagine what my roses will do in the hot sunshine of California or for that matter of Spain and other warm, sunny countries, how or whether they will flourish there as well as they do in temperate climates. Sometimes they flourish too much. A plant that would grow to about four feet high here, which I would call a big plant, like Uncle Walter (*facing page* 44), might grow to twelve or fifteen feet in a hot climate, and that would please no one. The aim is to breed roses that will be successful in all climates, as Herb Swim does in the U.S.A.— which includes our climate, too, for Portland, Oregon, has much the same weather as we have here in Britain. Swim breeds for roses with petals that will not fade or burn up in the hot sun, and which, when the flower is going over, will drop their petals cleanly. The foliage, too, must be durable in the heat.

In America they also have trouble in winter. In Britain you may plant a rose and it is nearly certain to take and to grow, and to endure the frosts, but in much of the U.S.A. it is not as easy and if you do not cover the plant with soil before the winter comes it will certainly be killed by frost. In the season, if it is not sprayed regularly, armies of leaf-bugs and root-bugs will kill it within a year.

The things we do not work for, I and other hybridists, are pink hybrid teas, because they appear in breeding lines anyway, and we do not work for white, because there is a limited demand for white. I do not work for single or semi-double floribundas either, because they would have to be exceptionally good to be at all popular. The market shows clearly enough that what people want are floribundas with blooms of hybrid-tea shape. I work for climbers of many kinds, and at present I am working on minia- tures. My idea for roses in my lifetime is that the gardener may order any colour he wants in any form—as a bush rose, as a climber, or as a miniature. I would do away with the terms 'hybrid tea' and 'floribunda'. Instead I would classify roses accor- ding to use—for house decoration, for garden display, for exhibi- tion, for climbing or rambling, for ground cover, for greenhouses. I think that this terminology will eventually prevail.

All these plants will have something like the hybrid-tea shape of bloom. The cross of the hybrid tea and the hybrid perpetual made a rose much more floriferous than either of its parents. Teas did not have enough vigour in themselves, but when crossed with the hybrid perpetuals they gave a plant that was much more hardy and much more floriferous, with a long flowering season. The hybrid teas brought a new and deeper interest in rose- growing. That was why my grandfather got off to a good start in his hybridizing, because hybrid teas were possible in our damp climate here in Northern Ireland. If they would grow here, in our weather, the hybrid teas could be guaranteed to grow almost anywhere.

We can look further back than the hybrid teas. The rose has been bred from very few species—'species' is the word rose-growers use for any kind of wild rose. Only eight or nine species have been used in the development of the modern rose, but there are dozens of other species that have not been used at all. It is exciting and invigorating to take something like that, which has not been bred from before, and incorporate it into the breeding line.

This is the place for a display of technicalities. The cells of a rose are each made up of a certain number of chromosomes in multiples of seven. Roses with 14 chromosomes are called diploid, that is they have 2×7 chromosomes. Other roses are triploid, with 3×7 or 21 chromosomes, others again are tetraploid, with 4×7 or 28 chromosomes. Occasionally one finds a hexaploid with 42 chromosomes. If a diploid is crossed with a tetraploid the result is a triploid. Most of the roses we would want to use are tetraploid. So, if we take a diploid and cross it with a tetraploid, what comes out is a triploid that will not cross with a tetraploid. The only way we can use that triploid is to cross it with a hexaploid in the hope that some of its progeny, if any, will become tetraploid and enable us to go on. But to do that can be a life's work for one man. This shows the complexity of the hybridizing business, and what happens when we use a species no one else has used. I have bred a rose called Maxi, coming out this year (1971), from a species hybrid known as *Rosa macrophylla coryana*, a large-leaved Chinese wild rose that is very resistant to black-spot. Everybody will start breeding from *macrophylla* now. Another example is Kordes' Frühlingsmorgen, which he bred from *Rosa spinosissima*, the Scotch briar or Burnet rose. He did not really get any farther with that. What breeders try to do is to break through on to a completely new line, and I was fortunate to do that with Picasso, which I bred from Kordes' Frühlingsmorgen. There are at present very few breeders working with species roses—I think only Swim, Kordes, and I are doing it to any

35

important extent. Nobody else seems to want the bother. For it is not a brief and simple business. On the contrary, it is a long job and in my lifetime I shall not see the end of it. It has taken me fifteen years to get my *macrophylla coryana* half-way tamed.

Macrophylla coryana is a rose that blooms once a year and grows up to fifteen feet tall. What I wanted to do with it was to tame it into a disease-resistant floribunda that would flower all the season with a bloom like that of a hybrid tea, and growing only four or five feet tall. The big problem is to break the once-flowering habit. If a once-flowering rose is bred with a hybrid tea or a floribunda, about 99·99 per cent of the seedlings will be once-flowering. So if there is a seedling that is at all perpetual, that is the one to continue with. The first repeat flowering seedling I got from *Rosa macrophylla coryana* grew eight feet tall, bolt upright, with a few miserable single rose-red flowers on top. But it did repeat.

The numbers can be astronomical. The odds against getting an acceptable rose, if you are trying for something specific, are about eight million to one; so if something promising, though unforeseen, turns up in the line you pursue that and the odds against success may be thereby reduced to two hundred thousand to one —better, but not what a gambler would be happy to accept. And it must be considered what all this means in terms of time. If in the first year luck and experience allow me to choose the right parents, it could take seven years, and would probably take longer, to produce a rose that would be a valuable addition to my catalogue and a reasonable seller. That is no doubt why there are so few rose-breeders in the business. It is not a question of crossing two roses and then waiting seven years for your new rose to appear. It is seven years or more of crossing roses year by year, seven years of inspecting seedlings and choosing right and crossing for more seedlings.

With time on this scale we have to come to talking of money. My breeding-house costs something in the region of £20,000 per year, so with seven years there is a cost of £140,000. If only one new rose came out in that time, that is the sort of investment it would represent, and the amount of money I would have to get back in sales before any profit appeared. But I have, of course, a progression of roses coming along all the time, and getting better each year, so that the capital investment is shared and revolving. Anyone who is starting rose-breeding from scratch, however, has to think of this size of investment and this length of time, and he would be highly unlikely to catch up with Poulsen, or Kordes, or Pat Dickson, or me. We would be generations ahead and getting farther ahead all the time. It will be seen from this that the most fortunate of rose-breeders is he who starts young with luck and lives long with hard work.

I have been at it now for some twenty years and I feel sometimes that I am only just starting, that only now am I beginning to understand. I am probably a good hybridist, but any excellence I have achieved is largely due to the fact that I started young, while others came into the business later in life. I would not call myself a real expert hybridist. I am just fortunate that I have been able to have those twenty years in the first part of my life, so that I have now gained as much experience and have had as much good fortune as older people who have been in the business longer than I have. I may be as good as other people are, but I am still learning and I hope to be a lot better ten years from now. After that very proper modesty I can go on to say that McGredy's nursery is probably the largest breeder of garden roses in the world. In its history McGredy's has produced 265 new varieties and 88 of those are mine.

I have had good roses because I am lucky enough to have good eyes for the job, but I know now that anyone who is going to earn the description of rose-breeder, of a consistent rose-breeder, that is, will have to work at it fifteen or twenty years. There is, of course, luck, fantastic luck, such as Alec Cocker in Scotland had when he chose the right parents first time and produced Alec's Red, a magnificent rose, from a cross of Fragrant Cloud and Dame de Cœur.

With luck like that you could become a rose-breeder on one acre of land, with 25,000 plants a year. Otherwise, you would keep those plants down for two years, and so also with the next crop, and you would need to have four or five acres with a third of an acre under glass, to breed roses the way I and other professionals are doing it. You would have to do your breeding indoors—even in California, in that warm climate, they do their breeding under glass—because you would have better control of the breeding stock and be able to keep insects away from it. Breeding *has* been done outdoors, with paper or polythene bags put over the fertilized roses, but that method does not give as many viable seeds as are obtained under glass, and the germination would not be as good.

You could have success in time if you dream the right dreams and have a good pair of eyes and the perception to see what is good in a seedling. Failure is just the opposite. It comes from choosing the wrong parents and choosing the wrong seedlings from them. For example, you could take the rose Mrs. Sam McGredy and you could cross it thousands of times and you would not get a decent seedling, despite the fact that in its day it was an outstanding rose. It has never produced a good pup. Another rose similarly bereft of decent progeny is Jan Spek (*facing page* 84). I have never had a seedling from this rose that was worth anything—all its seedlings were scrawny with blooms of a pale colour and with confused centres. I believe I could make a million crosses with Jan Spek and get nothing.

Rose-breeders use numbers to identify seedlings and usually these numbers give a hint of the amount of work involved. A number such as 69–2357, for instance, would indicate the 2,357th cross of 1969. When a promising line comes into being, however, I give the roses in it nicknames, usually nicknames derived from a group of related names, as in a family. Everybody in the nursery then uses these names, because in conversation names mean more than numbers and are more illuminating. I gave all the seedlings that led up to Picasso Spanish nicknames. Similarly, I had a strain of roses with the nicknames Good Morning, Good Evening, Good Afternoon, and so on. Then I had a series of motor-car nicknames.

The Spanish names for the family of Picasso included, Pépé, Tio, José, etc. Picasso itself, however, is not a great parent, yet I know that breeders everywhere are going to use it. It is Picasso's mother José that is the good parent, and José will never go on the market. Having a rose like that is what gives a breeder advantage. I must be making five thousand crosses each year from that one rose, and so I shall never sell it. Anyone else who wants to work in this direction will have to go through Picasso, which is José diluted by 50 per cent or more. Similarly Kordes had the good fortune to raise his *Kordesii* climber, which is frost-resistant. It was the result of a chromosome change, and now every year he breeds from it with all kinds of pollen.

I believe that most breeders use numbers first for their seedlings and then, later, go over to nicknames as we do, when they think they are coming closer to the mark. I could have five hundred roses in my fields and I would know them all by nicknames. I dream about them at night, under their nicknames. I have a series of seedlings called Moon Landing, Take-off, Safe Landing, Astronaut, Apollo, etc. There are series named after golfers and tennis players. I do not have to be told when the open golf championships are on or when tennis is being played at Wimbledon—it is when the roses are in bloom. So I have Rosewall, Hoad, Jacklin, and so on. Sometimes I use names in the news. I have seedlings called Macleod, Heath, Powell, Maudling, etc. I find it amusing that of these 'political' seedlings, the one with the most consistent colour was Powell. Eventually we put Powell on the market, but, with fine racial impartiality, under the name of Satchmo (*facing page* 116), after Louis Armstrong.

The shape of a rose, of the bloom, is something that may or may not be important. It is important that hybrid-tea roses should be high-pointed, with petals reflexing backwards. I believe that the more ovoid a rose is the worse it is. I like to see a rose with a high centre and the petals reflexing. I do not much care for big roses such as Red Lion or Red Queen. These are roses for the exhibitor, not for the garden. There is a Dutch rose called Anneke Doorenbos, after the daughter of a park superintendent—every bloom it produces is a hopeless flower, quartered and with two or three centres. The plant never gets any disease, however, but just flowers and flowers away without attention and that is why it is a good town-parks rose. As a parks rose it is planted in thousands because it is no bother. Anneke Doorenbos shows that shape is not everything. In the kind of market I breed for, I have to think of shape, but health is at least as important.

Habit, the form of the plant, is important too. Habit and vigour are allied. I have to think of special purposes, of 'horses for courses', that is. I find that there is a growing demand for roses of dwarf habit—for cushion roses. A rose-gardener can now buy the shape and kind of rose he wants for various purposes, and the important thing is that, for whatever purpose, the shape of the plant should be good; it should not, for instance, grow one-sided. Picasso, Sunday Times, and Kim are good examples of these shorter roses. In the U.S.A. Swim's 'Talk' series—Sweet Talk, Town Talk, etc.—are really popular.

The colour of a rose is a question of taste, but some preferences are clear. Deep yellow will always have the better, commercially, of pale yellow. That is why Peer Gynt has the measure of Grandpa Dickson. The most popular colour for a rose is undoubtedly scarlet red, followed by vermilion, followed by yellow, followed by pink, followed by white, with lavender and similar bluish roses coming last. Blue does not exist—not yet. A cerulean-blue rose, the colour one should mean by 'blue' in this context, will come only as the result of a distinct genetical change.

As far as colour is concerned, what I try to breed for, and it is important, is a good dying colour. The dying colour should be attractive until the petals fall. Some roses, especially some white ones, become the colour of brown paper, some go pale or bluish. Arthur Bell (*facing page* 76) is an example of a yellow rose that pales with a dying colour but is still yellow and pretty. Kronenbourg (*facing page* 72), on the other hand, is a perfect example of a rose beautiful in bud and in flower that goes a dreadful colour when it dies. It opens as a brilliant scarlet and gold, turns wine colour when it is going over, and dies purple.

Casino

I remember that we had a letter from a customer who wrote that he liked the colour of the buds of Kronenbourg he had from us and he liked the dying colour, but he did not like what came between, and he could not make up his mind whether he should remove all the blossoming flowers or take off all the buds—but he was sure the two should not come together.

Kordes' Pinocchio was the parent of Gene Boerner's Masquerade. Boerner was interested in Pinocchio because in this he had a rose that deepened in colour as it died, and this was one of the things he was looking for. It was pink and went out a reddish pink, and that was really why Boerner used it in further breeding —he liked to get a deeper dying colour in his roses. Ma Perkins is a good example because it starts as a pale pink and holds it, and then deepens a little. In short, Boerner sought reasonable colour stability. Masquerade was just fortuitous—he was not really looking for a yellow rose that would turn red as it grew older.

All the older roses and the inter-war roses paled in colour as they aged, and many modern roses do the same. Red roses have a tendency to turn a bluish colour, or they will look blue when the sky is overcast. An outstanding example of a rose that keeps its colour is Pharaoh by Meilland; it starts a fiery, fiery scarlet, and no matter what the weather does it dies a fiery scarlet. Unfortunately, though a wonderful colour, the plant is not free in its bloom. An opposite example is a rose called Fusilier, raised by Dennison Morey as a product of a huge nursery he inspected from a seat on a tractor. It won the All-America Award ten or twelve years ago. It did wonderfully in the sunny gardens of California, but in our cooler, less sunny climate, though the very tight bud was orange, before it was half open it was turning towards blue-red.

Colour stability in roses is at least as important as colour itself, but it is a question of compromise with all the other attributes we have to look for.

The recognition points of a good rose are several, but not all are plainly visible when the customer buys his plant. I put vigour first, with health and disease-resistance. Colour-stability, as I have said, is important in a modern rose, and so is repeat or continuous flowering. Fragrance is far down the line, mostly because it is very difficult to breed for it. If you breed for fragrance alone you lose too many other things. Fortunately—and it was mere chance —two of the greatest roses bred in recent times, Prima Ballerina and Spartan, are both highly fragrant. The fragrance has come through to their offspring Elizabeth of Glamis (*facing page 56*), Courvoisier, Mullard Jubilee, and Fragrant Cloud. In fact, there are a lot of fragrant roses now.

Amateur gardeners and rose-lovers will always say that fragrance is one of the most important characteristics in a rose but they do not carry that belief through into buying. Peace and Super Star are two of the best-selling roses in the world and neither of them is strongly fragrant. I know that the first thing anyone does when given a rose is to smell it, and they may be disappointed if there is no scent, but even if there is they do not translate their sensation or approval into purchase. There is a notion that all old roses were fragrant, but I am sure that this arises from certain old roses having been cherished for the sake of their fragrance while others have been allowed to die away. I am convinced that not more than 30 per cent of old roses were strongly fragrant, and I think the same percentage applies to modern roses.

Even with scented roses the question arises, what does the public want a rose to smell like? There is no such thing as a 'scent of roses'. Fragrance differs from variety to variety. We have roses that smell like apples, some like cinnamon, some like apricots or raspberries, some like tea or spices, others are lemony. Some roses smell like cheese, and that is neither expected in a rose nor pleasant, but there it is. It is possible to raise a seedling with a very good bloom but with a disgusting smell. We could not sell a rose like that—we would have to throw it away.

Occasionally I dream of breeding something more ambitious than roses. The ultimate in plant-breeding would be to breed trees, real trees that grow tall and live for a century or more. I have in mind a red horse-chestnut, *Aesculus carnea*—there are some fine specimens in Hyde Park in London and in Paris. Now, there is another very interesting variety of horse-chestnut, called *Aesculus indica*, which has creamy yellow flowers and blooms a month later than the *carnea*—in June, in fact. The dream would be to combine the desirable qualities of the two kinds, assuming they were fertile. I would gather pollen from the *indica* in June and keep it in the fridge until the following May, that is the following year, and then when the *carnea* came into bloom I would cross it with the *indica* pollen, and then I would plant all the seed that came from this cross. Ten years later I would have ten acres of seedlings coming into blossom and I would choose the trees that seemed most promising and cross them again and once more sow the seed, and wait another ten years for a repetition. I would keep planting and crossing like this until in about three hundred years, assuming that I could still be around and with my interest in horse-chestnuts undiminished, I might have hundreds of acres of chestnuts, and just a few of them, with luck, would have red or yellow or bicolour bloom going on continuously from May to June or July. It would be like reaching the moon, or, by then, perhaps the Andromeda nebula. It would be a great achievement but probably with no commercial value, a challenge accepted for the pure love and pride of succeeding. Nobody could do this other than some established family believing in its continuance through the next twelve or fifteen human generations, or a society confident of its endurance into the future.

People who know little about the rose business suppose that breeding and selling roses is an ideal job, all beautiful colour and fragrance, a romantic kind of job. That is purely illusion. There are interesting stories, of course, like that of Meilland and Peace, but there are harder realities, such as the occasion when some careless hand puts the wrong spray into a spraying-machine and kills off acres of roses—all one's business and profit gone for a year. Or times early in the year when a week of beautiful spring-like weather brings the roses on and a hard frost follows and kills all the buds. Or a year, like this year, when I have an unaccountable germination failure.

There are about three days in the year when life for me is absolute heaven, and those are when in summer the weather has been good for a time and has brought out the roses, and Niels Poulsen and Reimer Kordes would be here. We tell everyone who might worry us to go away and we make no plans for anything and don't see anybody—we just plod up and down through the rose fields up to our knees in blossoms, and we look at the seedlings. We do that for two or three days together. That is as close to a rose-man's heaven as you can get.

As for disappointments and regrets, the other side of the coin, there is of course Grandfather's famous pure-blue rose. It was probably a deep lavender, but nobody then had ever imagined a rose such as Lilac Time or Sterling Silver or Blue Moon or Silver Star, so his blue rose must have been very remarkable in his day. He probably had an unusual and outstanding lavender, which he was a fool to throw away, but there it was, he took that seedling, which would have put him thirty years ahead in that line, and threw it on a bonfire. We had to come back to it the hard way, and slowly we bred another bluish rose, a greyish blue, which was put on the market as Grey Pearl just before the war. That was a queer rose. In the nursery it was nicknamed the Mouse.

It was Gene Boerner who realized the value of Grey Pearl. He took a bush of it back to the U.S.A. and raised Lavender Pinocchio. A woman amateur raised Sterling Silver from an unnamed seedling and Peace. I think that the unnamed seedling must have been Grey Pearl or a rose from the same strain. Sterling Silver gave Tantau his Blue Moon, and from that came all the lavenders, all, I believe, out of Grey Pearl, which was unlikely to have been as good a blue rose as the one Grandfather threw away.

As for the truly blue rose, I suppose that today such a rose would be worth a million pounds. It might not look very well on the plant, but for cut-blooms it would be wonderful. Mixed with forsythia or yellow mimosa it would make a bouquet that would stagger anyone coming in view of it. Even lavender roses are splendid in such company. Some people wear lavender roses

Uncle Walter

in their buttonholes for their snob value or as a talking-point. Think what attention a blue rose could get!

I would say that a real blue colour, a sky-blue, is not at present possible. It could come, as I have already said, from a mutation, a change of genes, but we have not got the blue pigment in any rose at present. The gene for true orange was not in any rose, either, and now there are several oranges and orange scarlets because of the mutation that gave Kordes' Independence.

Rose-breeders cross female and male roses, and cross them back again in the quest for new varieties. Scientists say it makes no difference whether rose A is crossed with pollen from rose B, or rose B is crossed with pollen from rose A. I have had a lot of arguments about this. When I say it *does* make a difference the scientific people are amused. For example, Karl Herbst as a mother was never any good, but Karl Herbst as a father was so good it was known amongst us all as the 'Old Bull'.

Spartan as a mother was wonderful, but nothing much has come from Spartan as a father. I remember a long discussion at one of the international rose conferences when Professor Harland of Birmingham University declared that we were all mistaken on this question. Well, scientifically, we may all be wrong, but I doubt that there is a single rose-breeder who will agree that it makes no difference which parent in a cross supplies the pollen. It may be true of potatoes and cabbages and carrots—I don't know—but it certainly is not true in the practice of rose-breeding. However the crosses may be made, Herb Swim believes, and I agree with him, that good roses come only from good parents. Formerly I would have taken a rose with one particular characteristic I wanted to transmit but with fifteen bad characteristics I did not want, and I would breed from it for that one good characteristic. What happened was that I could get what I was after all right, but along with it came a lot of bad qualities, and then I had to spend years breeding those faults out. Now I follow Herb Swim's advice, because I know he is the master and I am happy to be his pupil.

An instance is a rose of Kordes' called Vienna Charm, a bronzy-coloured rose, with the kind of colour I think will be fashionable in the seventies. Vienna Charm has the colour, but it is a plant that is subject to die-back, black-spot, and mildew, and so on. Nevertheless, it has the colour and so it is used—Kordes has used it to produce Old Timer, a rose with a wonderful colour, but with so many faults it can be difficult to get it to grow at all. We will not introduce this rose here. It is good in California, however, where there is a long and dry growing season. The search for colour can lead into all kinds of trouble. This was the problem with yellow roses when they started—they were so prone to black-spot and die-back that they were difficult to grow. Gardeners learned to expect trouble with yellow roses.

In Grandfather's time there were no really good yellow roses. Yellow garden roses started only with Pernet-Ducher in the early 1900s. All grandfather had to work with or to sell were red, white, pink, and mauve roses. We can trace the colour yellow back, of course, to the Austrian Copper, *Rosa foetida*, which was a bicolour, and from it came Soleil d'Or about 1900. Soleil d'Or was a climber that had to be tamed down to a bush. When the yellow came in there came with it a lot of black-spot and lack of winter-hardiness, and it took more than half a century from Soleil d'Or in 1900 to breed those faults out. Now yellow roses are reasonably healthy and winter hardy.

Kordes raised Independence, a sealing-wax red, in 1950 and that gave birth to a race of orange roses. Some interesting roses may come from Zambra, the popular orange and yellow rose that Meilland raised and marketed in 1961. About the same time there was a beautiful rose called Golden Slippers, from Von Abrams, which it was hoped would start a new colour strain, but it did not produce any worthwhile progeny. Golden Slippers will grow well enough in the garden, but it will not produce good seedlings. Frensham was a little like that, too.

The trouble may lie in the chromosome count. To find out the chromosome count of a rose, scientists take a smear of the plant, preferably of the growing tip of a shoot, where it is easier to see what is multiplying and dividing to produce new cells, in other words, is actively growing. If a rose proves to be a triploid with 21 chromosomes, we know we have something difficult to breed from. It is a question of the division of the number. In straightforward breeding a rose takes half its chromosomes from one parent and half from the other and when there is a question of an odd number, such as twenty-one, I suppose that a fight goes on to see which will get the odd chromosome and the result is that nothing comes out.

Another thing with which we have a lot of trouble is colour description. The standard we might go by is the Royal Horticultural Society's colour-guide, which is a colour-fan of graduated colours from dark to light through the rose spectrum. We have to use this colour-guide when we make out a specification for a rose patent, but it is not used in catalogues for the general public. One reason is that few customers would have the R.H.S. colour-guide, and another is that all roses change colour throughout the life of the flower, either paling or deepening. There is the question of what stage you would describe a rose, and whether the description would mean anything to the average gardener. For patent applications we describe a rose at three stages—bud, fully open, and spent. A patent description would read something like this: 'Front of petals red 5A graded yellow 3R, overlaid red 6A—Reverse of petals yellow 3D.'

When you have produced a good rose and entered it for trials there is excitement, a thrill in winning an award, a jump of the heart when you know that you have won. It is not quite what it was for me, because I have now won so much that I have become a bit blasé, but I do not mind being beaten any more. I used to take it to heart if I was beaten. Since I have won almost everything in the rose world, I can now get pleasure out of seeing someone else win the awards. For example, to see Alec Cocker win the President's Trophy in 1970 was delightful, almost as much pleasure for me as it was for him. Nevertheless it would still be fun, and rather grand, to do a grand slam again or win on a climber. A grand slam is to win all the European awards, or those that count, with one rose—as Mullard Jubilee did.

I am excited about Mullard Jubilee (*facing page* 120), which has also won the top American award this year. That is a really good rose that is going to be worth a lot of dollars in the next ten years. That money will pay for a lot of future rose-breeding, at least to carry me along some of the way until I get another world-class rose, which I shall need at latest about 1980. I know I have that rose as a seedling out in my fields now. A breeder produces perhaps five or six top-class roses in a lifetime if he keeps going as long as I hope to keep going. I have had Piccadilly, for example, and Elizabeth of Glamis (*facing page* 56), and Mullard Jubilee, and now I have that priceless seedling coming along and I think that it is going to be better than any of the others. That seedling is going to win a lot of awards.

I also have a pot-rose coming along now, a miniature, that I think is good and I am sure I shall win some awards with it. That will give me joy because no one has done it before. Picasso gives me pleasure, too, because it is a novel kind of rose. It has come out this year, and its chances are very good.

I'm a bit blasé about travel also, because I have done and still do so much of it, going to rose exhibitions and shows and to other breeders and propagators to see what they are doing that might be competitive. I think that all we rose-breeders travel a lot, and part of that is due to a desire to check up on our roses grown under licence in foreign countries, under the plant patents regulations. In any nursery I can see at a glance approximately how many McGredy roses a propagator is growing, and so I get an idea of his business and a rough check on what I ought to receive in royalties. In one country I had to use a lawyer, who found that I was being underpaid by as much as £5,000 per year. He stopped that and got the backlog too. Most breeders travel in Europe to trials three or four times every year, and then we travel to visit each other and each other's nurseries. I go to Kordes' every year, and he comes here. The same with Spek, Dickson, etc. I go to France perhaps half a dozen times annually, to plant-breeders' meetings that are for the most part connected with plant protection, with guarding our rights in different countries, or trying to get those rights extended, to include cut-blooms, maybe, or to cover trade marks. These meetings are in the language of the country, with French, German, and English translations going on at the same time through earphones. We find at these meetings that there is a lot of camaraderie. Many of us have the same hobbies or games, and it is a strange fact that rose-breeders are nearly all music-mad, we are all more or less lovers of fine food (that is not surprising), and we all love bathing in saunas or steam baths.

Nurseries vary in character quite a lot. Here in Northern Ireland what I have now is a unified horticultural farm of over 200 acres. That is not common. Poulsen's nursery is hidden away and difficult to find and he does not get a lot of visitors; he does business by parks superintendents coming to his nursery and by sending out catalogues. Kordes' nursery is a field here, a field there, a field somewhere else, mostly rented. He produces a map showing the location of his fields and you have to drive around Sparrieshoop to find them.

All rose-breeders, of course, get visitors who come just to see the spectacle. They like to walk through the fields enjoying the roses, and we let them come in; but we keep them away from the seedling field, because there they might do a lot of damage, even if they accidentally destroyed only one plant—it might be the very plant that could be the parent of a new variety.

Rose-breeders are a small group, but, wandering round the world as we do, we are always running into each other. We visit each other in our homes, and carry each other's roses in planes to rose-shows, and we prefer even to wear another breeder's rose in a buttonhole rather than one of our own. I am godfather to Niels Poulsen's daughter, and every one of us is known as 'uncle' to the others' children. The previous generation was the same. My Uncle Walter was a close friend of Uncle Svend Poulsen.

There are fashions in roses as in everything else, but as the genesis of a new rose is such a long period fashions have to move more slowly than in other things. In the past we have had tea roses giving place to hybrid perpetuals, and those in turn to hybrid teas. Polyanthas earned a place, only to lose it to floribundas. Colours too have their vogue. I think that the fashion for the future is going to favour the orange and ochre colours and the trend will be towards a purpose rose—as I have remarked earlier we shall stop talking about hybrid teas and floribundas and more about roses for purposes—for climbing, for cutting, for beds or for pots, all available with matching colours and blooms. I believe, too, that my 'hand-painted' series will become fashionable. I have worked hard to bring out Picasso, and this is certain to be followed by other roses of this kind.

It used to be the case that new fashions would begin from flower-shows, where new roses were first seen by the public. Flower-shows used to be one of the main contacts between rose-breeders and the public, and they were also places where an order might be placed. The Chelsea Flower Show is the one that springs first to mind. But times have changed; not many people now place orders at shows. Our orders from Chelsea have dropped from £7,000 to £1,500 over the last five years. We do not go to the shows to get orders any more, but rather use them to show the flag and to meet some of our friends among the public.

Among the pleasant surprises I have found is the unexpected success of climbing roses. Not long ago most breeders would have considered climbers not the kind of roses to go nap on, but I have and I have been delighted with the response.

A disaster is when flowers do not turn up at a show to which they have been dispatched in good time. One of the most annoying accidents was when a sulphur burner I have in a greenhouse to control mildew went on fire one night and wiped out tens of thousands of seedlings. Another time a careless hand put the wrong spray mixture into a spraying-machine and destroyed £20,000 worth of standard roses.

The trouble going on in Northern Ireland at the present time is certainly a disaster, for the public and incidentally for us too.

People identify roses with pleasant things, and if something unpleasant is going on they do not buy. All the nurseries in Northern Ireland have been hurt by this. We have had sufficient people phoning us up, asking if we are still in business, to know that hundreds of others, probably thousands, just do not phone. Even when they do know that we are still breeding and selling, they wonder if they will get their roses or whether the post office will be burned out or something of the sort. They want to buy more roses, but they cannot imagine what is going on here. In fact the troubles are confined to very small areas mostly in only two cities, and there is no reason why roses we dispatch should not reach the people they are addressed to.

When I started in the business I used to think that British roses were always the best, and in a sense they are, because they have been bred in and for our climate. In those days the important nurseries were in the United Kingdom—Wheatcroft and Gregory, Harkness and Mattock, and Dickson and McGredy's; we were all substantial firms and well known. In Europe I had heard of Kordes, getting on his feet again after the war, and the Poulsens from back in the thirties, and then suddenly Meilland burst on the scene and began to wipe the floor with the lot of us and with the Americans too.

The Americans were the first to have plant patents and that fact encouraged the rise of mass hybridization techniques in the States, of the techniques of the modern rose-breeding business. We in Britain rather emulated them than they us, but we got into big business too, and while none of us in Europe could individually match Jackson & Perkins' output, the total of our trade is not now a lot below the American figure; I think that British propagators grow about fifty million roses every year, and the U.S.A. about sixty million.

Nurseries are not large employers of labour, though they may employ more men than an ordinary farmer with the same extent of land. I employ about eighty people. There are various grades of pay in any nursery. A budder is paid a skilled rate; he is what we call a 'knife-man'. Anyone who can use a knife properly is paid more than someone who cannot use a knife. A budder deals with putting the buds on to the species understock, and he also does occasional grafting. On top of that a budder is paid a percentage based on the number of successful buddings he does. A record is kept for every man. Up to 81 per cent he gets a bonus of fifty-five pence per thousand, and for 90 per cent or more successful buddings he gets a pound per thousand. In some nurseries the budders are paid a bonus on the number of buddings they do in a day, and they may bud up to four thousand plants daily. I do not like that because if they did two thousand or more a day, I could find that increased speed brings with it less careful work and I might be paying a bonus for a poor crop. Here the men achieve a speed of about thirteen hundred buddings a day. We are, however, trying a limited system of bonus on numbers budded in 1971.

At Portadown we bud on *multiflora* seedling understocks, with stems five-eighths of a centimetre thick. I think *multiflora* seedlings give better plants, but *multiflora* seedlings are not as easy to bud as are *mutliflora* cuttings, which are used in America. We bud in the field on one-year seedlings that have naturally grown a kinky neck. In California they take cuttings and stick them in the ground to root. The stems stay very straight and consequently are much easier to bud, and that is why they are able to achieve such a large output. We could not use cuttings because of our lack of sun, but in California they root their cuttings to about 98 per cent success. To conserve the moisture in the ground, for the cuttings to take, they put down long ribbons of paper and stick the cuttings through this. The paper helps to keep the soil moist and it keeps down the weeds.

Our men are members of the Transport and General Workers' Union. The district organizer, Tom Ferron, is a very able man. His is a tough union, tough on both sides, on me and on the men, but it is fair and considerate. I do not think that they would support an unofficial strike, but they would bring the men out tomorrow if they thought that I was being unfair. Paddy Murphy is the senior shop-steward and Mick Creany is the junior shop-

School girl

steward. The union bitches, of course, like any other, and I bitch at them at times, too, but there is no such thing as a restrictive practice here. The union will consider anything at any time, anything we want to do to improve productivity.

In the summer I used to have fifty or sixty schoolboys pulling out weeds between the roses and then in every field we used to have horses drawing grubbers up and down between the rows to make a fine tilth. It was supposed that a fine tilth kept the plants growing well. But in wet weather, that fine tilth became thick soup and walking along the rows was a muddy trudge. Today the schoolboys come no more and the horse and the grubber have gone too. We spray a weed-killer called Simazine on the ground. This weed-killer is one of the best improvements in my lifetime. My father and my grandfather would without doubt be shocked if they could see that harrowing for a fine tilth is no longer done. Today, I have not got a pair of boots and do not need them; I walk along the rows in old but ordinary shoes.

The method of budding has some variations in different countries. Whatever you do, you have to get down low to bud a rose. Some Californians use a trolley made of planks and cycle wheels. The man using one of these lies on his belly with a piece to support his forehead, and he kicks the contraption along with his feet. Of course, it is usually dry there. That method in Portadown would mean a soaking.

Our method of budding needs three men. One man goes along the row scraping the earth away from the base of the plant—he is called a 'hooker'. Then comes the budder, who makes a T-cut in the base of the stem of the understock and inserts the bud. He is followed by a man who ties the bud on—or used to tie it on—nowadays he uses what are called Fleischauer ties, which are rubber patches with prongs on. These ties simply wrap round the stem over the bud and snap on with the prongs. A child could do it. We have tried having two men budding and one man tying for the two, but it produces worse work and some confusion. The rubber patch goes on simply and covers the bud, but it rots off in about six weeks, when the bud should have taken. A larger and stronger tie is used for standard roses, which we bud on *rugosa* stocks. At the end of the year the head of the understock plant is cut off above the bud. A year later the budded rose is ready for sale.

Here we have a good staff to do the budding in the fields, mostly long-term employees. Those new to the job can be distinguished at once because when the first sunny day comes they take off their shirts, and if you are working with your back bent all day, you get burnt—very painfully burnt. Even in our soggy climate there is enough sun at times to burn the hide off the unwary. The wise ones, those with more experience, keep their shirts on and tie handkerchiefs round their heads.

We do not have many women in the nursery. In England and on the Continent women are emancipated, but not here, not just yet. It was a sensation here a few years ago when a Danish girl, a student, came over to work in the nursery for a while. At other times we have young men from the Continent coming as students; apart from these our labour is Irish. Here in Ireland we are able to get the labour we need because there is 10 per cent unemployment in this country, and men want jobs. We are not allowed to bring in foreigners as long as there is an Irishman available. Anybody, it seems, can get into England, but no one, not even the English, can come here unless there is a job waiting for them and there is no Irishman who can do it. That is why you do not see many coloured people in Portadown or Northern Ireland. The only coloured people here are self-employed—Indians in the rag trade, for example. In Portadown we have less than a dozen Pakistani and Indian families in a population of 20,000, and as for West Indian Negroes, I know of none.

There is another reason why we are in a happy position for labour. The average Irishman, an Englishman might suppose, is perverse and peculiar. He only wants to have enough money to go and have a good time, and then come back to work for the next occasion. Then again, many Irishmen, the kind of men who work in this nursery, do not want to work inside. Some of them occasionally go off to labour in a factory such as Goodyear's, and in three months they are aching to get out on the land again. It is that kind of mentality that keeps in being all the little, unproductive farms you find all over Ireland, north and south. The Irishman likes the open-air life, and sometimes when I have a lot to do that keeps me in my office I feel the same urge and I envy those men out in the fields and in the fresh air.

In winter, of course, it can be cold and miserable working in the fields, but the men have protective clothing for that kind of weather. In the farm buildings they all have heated lockers. When the men have been out in the fields and have got wet and cold they can come in and have a hot shower and put on dry, warm clothes. In my grandfather's days, I am told, and before him, the men went straight home after the day's work, in their wet clothes, and sat steaming by a turf fire.

We are following the American pattern in providing showers and locker facilities for the men who work here. Even when I was at school in the U.S.A. in 1948, most workers came home in the evening and first of all had a wash and changed their clothes. It is only in the last few years that the same could be said of Northern Ireland. Of course, it does not happen everywhere yet, because the facilities are not there. I see the results of the trend in my pub, the Craigavon Inn, where the customers have been home and changed before coming out for the evening. It is rare now to have a man coming into the inn straight from his work.

This changing from work clothes would not happen, perhaps, in the north of England, nor does it happen in the tougher parts of Belfast. But it is coming. One of the good effects of the Teddy-boy period and of Carnaby Street has been an increased clothes consciousness in the young. They want to look their best, according to their lights, when they go out in the evening or at the week-end.

In most countries of the world, nurseries employ immigrant labour. In Germany nearly all the labour is provided by Spaniards. Kordes has Spaniards coming to him in March and leaving in

December. They save up to go home for three months. Poulsen in Denmark is using Turks. In the U.S.A. white men did the budding first, and then negroes came in to do it. Incidentally, Texas negroes bud sitting down rather than bending down. Their method is to put a wooden plank along a row of under-stocks and bend several plants over with it at once, to reveal the lower stems where the buds are to go. Then they sit on the board and bud between their knees, sliding along the wood from plant to plant. However it is done, budding is a tiresome and difficult business, and when some other easier job turns up the budders are tempted to leave. When the negroes left, Mexicans moved in, but they too are now leaving the job and I hear that Chinese come from Hong Kong now to do budding in the U.S.A.

I have not much experience of budding—I do not suppose I have budded five hundred roses in my life. I just say what is to be done. The only training I have had was at Slocock's in Woking. It was in the winter, when the orders were being dis-patched and a large part of my time was spent in doing up parcels, in burning fruit trees that remained unsold, and in chopping bits of firewood for the foreman's house. Most other rose-growers have done everything in the nursery, have practical experience of all operations, but I am one of the few who has not. Certainly the Wheatcrofts, from Harry down, have all done it. So have the Dicksons. The only side of the business that I have gone through from A to Z is the plant-breeding side.

I must not omit to mention Ginger McKeown, who is sixty-two and has been here man and boy. He has a marvellous eye for a rose and is my right-hand man in the fields. I have two key people in the rose-breeding department. Pat Judge does the actual pollinating in the greenhouse, where he takes a firm line with me in the matter of greenhouse selection. Harry McKeown, or Ginger McKeown, is the key man in the rose fields, and he does the field selection with me. We walk side by side all day. I find that I have to have someone to talk to when I am selecting roses, someone to chat with and to swop opinions with, and Ginger is that man in the rose fields. I depend on him a lot. I would not

Elizabeth of Glamis

go, for example, to judge the Royal National Rose Society trials at St. Albans without Ginger. I would always bring him with me because together we do the job twice as well. The interesting thing is that he is the one man in the nursery to whom everyone will go. Niels Poulsen goes looking for Ginger as soon as he arrives. Reimer Kordes knows him and honours and respects his opinions. All the rose-breeders know Ginger McKeown, just as all the breeders are beginning to know Jochem, Reimer Kordes' number two. Ginger McKeown, for whom I have great affection, is internationally known for his knowledge of roses—in fact anybody who has a good eye for a rose soon becomes internationally known. One reason is that there are very few such people.

As in the case with other breeders, I enter my roses for rose-trials in various centres throughout the world. The most important, most highly regarded, are the trials of the Royal National Rose Society at St. Albans. Their awards are the most difficult to win, and therefore are those that every breeder most aspires to win. The rose that wins a gold medal, or better, the President's Trophy, has to be a good rose in every respect, a rose that other breeders are bound to admire because it must have so many good qualities. But the awards are no guarantee of sales. It is up to the breeder to go out and sell his prize-winning rose wherever he can, and it does not always follow that it will sell easily or well. For example, Dickson won the trophy with Grandpa Dickson in 1965. Grandpa Dickson is a magnificent rose of a light yellow colour—but just about that time, or a little later, Kordes brought out Peer Gynt, which is not quite as good as Grandpa Dickson but is a deep, deep yellow, and the deeper yellow is always what the public prefers.

The British trials are judged by impartial experts, and so are the Continental ones. The All-America Award, however, is different. It is organized by a society of nurserymen, and the rose that wins—as Mullard Jubilee recently won—gets the backing of the trade throughout the U.S.A. That is why I am confident that Mullard Jubilee is going to make thousands of dollars in the next few years. The men who judge the All-America trials know

E

what is required in a rose to make it a commercial success and of course they judge accordingly. If a large pink hybrid tea wins the award in one year, then another large pink hybrid tea is not likely to win the following year, though it may be a superlative rose, because the market will not take two such roses in consecutive years.

It is difficult for a foreigner to win the award, partly for this reason, and partly because roses have to be entered or sponsored by American nurserymen and this may be costly. So I do not do it unless I am very certain I have a winner. The All-America Award is the only one, except perhaps Nord-Rose in Scandinavia, that practically guarantees sales.

Nord-Rose is organized by a society of Scandinavian nursery-men that has its headquarters in Unnaryd in Sweden. The secretary is a Dane called Reider Haggard, who is always having to tell people that he is no relation of the author of *She*. The Nord-Rose selection committee takes cognizance of the rose-trials in Copenhagen in Denmark and visits them to see how the roses are coming along. Any rose that wins the Copenhagen gold medal is considered for the Nord-Rose award, but it does not follow automatically. The question is, will that rose sell? I have won numerous Nord-Rose awards, and that is partly because my roses are bred in the north and are especially suitable for northern temperate climates such as Scandinavia has. Piccadilly, Mullard Jubilee, Paddy McGredy, Mischief (*facing page* 20), have all won, and some others have won also. Pat Dickson got one with Grandpa Dickson.

Trial grounds in Europe cost us nothing, nothing that is beyond the value of the roses we have to send there. Occasionally a trial authority has proposed a charge, but we have resisted that through our plant-breeders' organization. The plant-breeders would boycott any trials that charged a fee, and that trial-ground would find itself with no plants to try.

One of the tasks that occasionally falls to the lot of a rose-breeder is to act as judge at a flower-show or rose-trial. It is usually a pleasant thing to do as long as no roses of one's own are entered. One judging occasion has left a deep mark on my memory. It was in Japan. In the West a judge is called upon to select the first three or the first four roses out of many on the basis of a display of the blooms or of the growing plant. The Japanese system is to show one rose only, in a narrow vase, and what I had to do was not to select the first three or four for awards, but to put all of fifty exhibits in order of merit. I began by putting what I thought was the best one on the right and the worst on the left and then I shuffled the remaining forty-eight roses back and forth with no convincing display of certainty, watched the while by all fifty competitors standing behind me. I was working roses to left and to right, and changing them again, and every time I moved one up or moved one down there was a sharp and unnerving gasp from behind me.

4. THE PRINCIPAL ROSE-BREEDERS
AND SOME NOTABILITIES OF THE ROSE BUSINESS

The breeding of roses is mostly a personal business and a family business and nurseries tend to pass from father to son and so to stay in one family. Some nurseries have flourished and have later for one reason or another ceased to exist, and that happened to several when the world-wide rose mail-order recession of the sixties, first in the U.S.A. and then in Europe, hit many of us very hard. But most of the principal breeders have survived. There never were very many, and the breeders and their families all know each other and get together at times, and visit each other in their homes. We are all friends, though we compete in business and each tries to outdo the other.

The reason why there are so few rose-breeding families is that rose-breeders are born rather than made. No kind of university study or university degree can make anyone a good rose-breeder if he does not have the gift.

When I started in roses, the U.S.A. breeders were at their peak. Largest of them all was the family firm of Jackson & Perkins, controlled by the Perkins brothers and their hybridist Gene Boerner. America having had plant patents since 1930, there has for a large number of years been an incentive there to breed roses, and as a result the Americans were way ahead of everybody else. Then, again, they were able to continue breeding roses during the last war, when many of us in Europe had to grow food. J. & P. was a rose colossus, with an enormous amount of money to spend, and it sank a lot of capital in the breeding of roses. The firm is probably best known for the development of the floribunda rose. The polyantha rose, a cluster-flower rose, was produced by Poulsen in Denmark in the 1920s. Gene Boerner refined it by putting a better shape of flower on it, and the result was called a 'floribunda'—the name is an American invention that caught on. It is technically incorrect, but that is not important now, because it is used everywhere. Boerner raised some magnificent roses, including Fashion, the first of the salmon floribundas, and a world-beater. About the same time he raised Masquerade, a rose that changes colour on the bush from yellow to red as it opens. Both of these roses came from Pinocchio, a medium-pink from Kordes of Germany, and not exceptional. Boerner was more imaginative in his use of Pinocchio than was Kordes, and Boerner got the break. A surprising thing, especially where there was so much money invested, was that Boerner did not have the same kind of success with hybrid tea roses as with floribundas. In all his time he bred only two hybrid teas of real quality. One is the yellow Diamond Jubilee, which came in 1947, and the other is Serenade, in 1950, a bright orange. Together with these successes he produced a lot of comparatively poor hybrid teas, nothing like as good as his string of floribundas. Towards the end of his life he concentrated on greenhouse roses. He brought to the U.S.A. a German floribunda raised by Tantau, called Garnette. Boerner was fascinated by this rose, and bred from it a series of greenhouse roses that came to be known as Garnette roses. The important thing about these Garnette roses was that they lasted a long time in the greenhouse or in a vase. True, the floribunda heads of bloom had to be disbudded to give one smallish flower per stem, but Garnettes would last for two weeks in water and these varieties made the rose a real competitor in the cut-flower business with carnations and chrysanthemums. Just before his death five or six years ago Boerner produced a Garnette rose that he called Zorina, an orange floribunda that is today the best of all the Garnettes.

I remember being with Gene Boerner in London one day. He went into a flower-shop and bought some red and pink Garnettes and put them in his brief-case—and that is no way to treat a rose!

Next day he gave a talk to the International Rose Convention, and to illustrate it he said: 'I bought some Garnette roses in a shop yesterday and put them in my brief-case, as Sam McGredy will tell you, for he was with me. The roses haven't been out of my brief-case since.' He put his hand into the case and took out the roses and shook them a bit, and they were perfect. Now what other rose could you do that with? Another trick of Boerner's, when anyone argued with him about the fragrance of a rose, was to take the rose and put it under his hat on his head, under the black Homburg he always wore. Then he would walk around the fields for a while, and eventually he would take off his hat, and the warmth had brought out the fragrance and made it stronger and more emphatic.

Boerner was a bachelor and lived in Newark in New York State—a little town, not the big Newark in New Jersey. His hobby was breeding dogs, especially dachshunds. (That reminds me that my father and my grandfather bred dogs too, but in their case it was fox-terriers. My father bred budgerigars and parakeets as well.) Gene was born and lived his early years in Wisconsin, where the botanic gardens at Hale's Corners bear the family name. He was very proud of his German ancestry, so much so that one of his greatest pleasures was to name a pink floribunda Frankfurt after the city of his forebears. He understandably was very close to the Kordes, where he was always 'Uncle Gene'.

Jackson & Perkins was controlled by the Perkins brothers. There were three of them, plus Gene, and together they built up the biggest and most powerful firm in the rose business. They could do anything they wanted and thought nothing of spending half a million dollars to promote a rose—as they did with Spartan, for example. Nobody in Europe could match them for quantity. Nobody on this side of the Atlantic could think of sending out so many millions of catalogues. They budded twenty million roses a year.

Charlie Perkins was a rough-diamond sort of character. He would come into a restaurant straight from the fields with his muddy boots on, sit down at the table, take out a cigar and bite the end off and spit it out on the floor. But he was wonderful in the rose-fields. He was transformed. One of my great pleasures was to spend a day with him walking up and down his rows of seedlings. Some of the seedlings would be mine or Kordes' and I would recognize them. I liked to get his opinions on how our roses would perform in the U.S.A. He might have seen them only in California and New York, where roses grow quite differently than they do in a cooler climate, but he could say quite accurately how they must have grown in Europe. That illustrates the ability of the man to select a rose that was right and know how it would perform in a very different climate thousands of miles away. And that was just by looking at the bloom and the quality of the plant as it grew on his land. He would back his judgement with a lot of money. He introduced and sold a lot of our roses in the U.S. before the second world war.

When I started to breed roses Gene Boerner showed me great kindness and helped me in many ways. I enjoyed my visits to his home near Newark and each year he came to look at the roses in Portadown. Unfortunately, these visits never resulted in business contracts and towards the end of his career I had the feeling that he was getting just a little jealous of his protégé. The break between us finally came at the International Gartenbau Ausstellung in Hamburg in 1961. I had chartered my own plane to Hamburg, filled it with roses, and set off to challenge the Germans in their own bailiwick. I was proud and happy to win a fair share of the prizes, particularly in the new roses section. Gene was there. He came over and sat down by my stand. 'Some day you're going to be a good rose-breeder,' he said. That remark made me angry, for his own varieties had not been particularly successful at the show, and he obviously had no intention of doing anything with mine in the U.S.A. I stomped off in a great temper. The first person I met was rose-breeder Bob Lindquist of Hemet, California. I asked him if he would be interested in any of my roses for the U.S.A. His enthusiasm made me change my agency from J. & P. that day. The result is that Bob will introduce Electron (Mullard Jubilee) in 1972 as the best rose in America. It takes such a long time to raise a new rose to bring fruit to such an agreement.

The Perkins brothers and Boerner all died or retired about the same time, and Jackson & Perkins was sold to a firm called Harry & David, who run it now on a smaller scale. The whole business was moved from Newark to California. Their new hybridist is Bill Warriner. He has inherited that most difficult kind of footwear—a dead man's shoes. At Rose Hills, a crematorium in southern California, I had the opportunity to see some of his latest seedlings in May 1971. I had better explain that this particular crematorium has one of the best rose-gardens in the U.S.A. Some of the best roses in the garden were Bill's. I was with Herb Swim at the time. We just looked at each other, saying, 'Oh, oh, here comes some tough competition!'

The other American companies are much smaller than Jackson & Perkins, but some of them are three times as big as mine here in Ireland.

My friendship with Californian Bob Lindquist dates back well before that I.G.A. Hamburg show. His record as a hybridist is formidable, with several All-America winners to his credit, including Granada, Tiffany, and Command Performance. His selection methods, however, do not suit our Irish climate very well, and many of his varieties have trouble surviving our damp weather. In the hotter climates of the U.S.A. and southern Europe they are splendid. Bob is a partner in the firm of Howard of Hemet. Paul, Chuzz, and Chuck Howard are all active in the firm, which includes one of the most enormous container-grown plant businesses I have seen. Huge trucks ferry all kinds of conifers and shrubs, growing in up to ten-gallon cans, throughout the U.S.A. In their nursery the lines of plants stretch as far as the eye can see. Bob modestly admits to having grown many acres of grapefruit and being president of a bank as well. Party-time at the Lindquist home is something to see. Ellie (Mrs. Lindquist) really sets up a party! Everyone starts from the kitchen, where Bob mixes a mean Margarita in the kitchen blender. This Tequila-Cointreau-lime-and-salt concoction is a knock-out, sometimes leading to a lot of cooling-off in the Lindquist pool.

Not far to the north of Hemet lives Herb Swim, the best hybridist of them all. Now, I consider myself very lucky that Herb Swim changed his job three times. He started off in rose-breeding with the Armstrong Company and he did wonders for them, raising, among others, Circus and Montezuma, but he left when one of the younger Armstrongs joined the firm from college and there seemed to be no future for Herb Swim. Now to have to leave a company like that is a disaster for a hybridist, because the breeding-stock, the roses he has selected and grown to provide pollen and seed, does not belong to him and he has to leave it behind and start again. He has access to any roses that have been put on the market from his hybridizing, of course, but not to the original breeding-stock, which is never sold. So he has to start again to build up another breeding-stock before he can produce any new roses. Herb Swim joined a man called Weekes, who had a nursery in California and who considered himself lucky, as indeed he was, to get the services of such a great hybridist. The new roses Swim would bring out were to be known as Weekes & Swim roses or Swim & Weekes roses. So Herb Swim started off again from scratch and within ten years he was producing roses like Oklahoma and Mr. Lincoln and winning awards right and left. Then the Armstrong Company realized that it was not doing very well without Swim, so they bought him back, and there was a repetition of the loss of breeding-stock and the need to start again. Now Swim is breeding beautiful roses once more. If he could have been able to carry on in that one job from the beginning, working away from the basis of a fine breeding-stock, with his flair for breeding roses he would have been an unapproachable giant—none of us would have been able to reach his heights.

Swim raised some fascinating Soulieana hybrids while with Weekes. These were the basis for a new kind of short, stubby, Erica-type roses. I believe they may have been destroyed since he left. If so, what a waste! He bred peaches too, and some of them were good, especially a little dwarf called Bonanza. He came over to Ireland about four years ago, and that visit remains bright in my memory. I cleared the decks to receive him, wouldn't have anybody or anything interrupt us. Niels Poulsen was here too and the three of us spent a marvellous day down in the rose-fields. We were like little sandboys together. We found that we bred roses in quite different ways. Herb was breeding roses to do their best in hot sunshine conditions, and Niels and I for the wetter and more temperate climates of Britain and Denmark.

An interesting aside—just after Herb rejoined Armstrongs', he and I together inspected the acres and acres of seedlings under test there. Herb was trying to pick up the strings again, taking on a strain that was not his. We walked along silently, looking at tens of thousands of varieties. After the last plant had been seen I said dispiritedly but frankly that in all those acres there was only one rose there on that day that pleased me—two plants of a bright red. 'Interesting,' said Herb. 'That's just about my feeling too.'

One of the most endearing of rose-breeders, now retired, is Walter Lammerts. He is particularly famous for one rose that is perhaps the most popular floribunda of all, a big, tall, blowzy rose that you see in nearly every garden in England. It is called the Queen Elizabeth rose, after the present Queen. It is remarkable how easily he got permission to use this name. If we in this country want to use a royal name, we have to undergo—and quite rightly—a very strict examination, as I had to when we wanted to call a rose of mine Elizabeth of Glamis (*page 56*). I was eventually given permission, and we have the letter framed in the office, typed with the giant typewriter that always seems to be used for royal correspondence.

Walter Lammerts has a university degree—he is a trained and qualified geneticist and he is very scientific. I sometimes find it difficult to understand him. I have been through the seedling fields with Walter on several occasions and I enjoy his company immensely, but I just do not know what he is talking about. The only man I know who can converse on his level is another American rose-breeder called Dennison Morey.

A few years ago I went with Maureen to the United States and among the people we visited were Walter Lammerts and his wife Maxine. We were just about to go into his house when—honest to God—I felt I had to flatten myself on the ground as a roaring Dakota went over at the height of the chimney. Lammerts' house was immediately at the end of an airfield flight-path, and he would sit there and curse the aircraft constantly—always swearing that he was going to do something about the noise. He took us out to a famous night-club called Bimbo's, and Maureen and I, who were young and thought ourselves vigorous, were amazed by Walter and his wife jitterbugging and twisting all night long. They had us beaten for energy.

I have already mentioned Dennison Morey. He worked for Jackson & Perkins in California, on the West Coast, but never got on with Gene Boerner and when old Charlie Perkins died the first thing Boerner did was to fire Morey. Now Dennison at Jackson & Perkins was an example of a geneticist with unlimited money at his disposal, unlimited training, and vast areas of land—he literally had hundreds of acres to every two of mine. He had so many rows of roses in his fields that when Gene went to California to inspect he could not walk them as I do mine. Gene and Dennison would sit on the back of a tractor and be towed up and down the rows so that they could see what the roses were doing. It was really too big a spread, a blunderbuss way of breeding roses, but out of this enormous number of plants Denny got a few really good ones. Probably the most notable is King's Ransom, a yellow hybrid tea. Many European breeders with only a small fraction of the capital Morey had at his command have done better, however, and that is because they not only have had eyes to see but also have had time to walk among their roses and to study them.

Denny, now on his own, has one particular seedling called Temple Bells, which I am putting on the market for him in Britain. Scientifically, it is most interesting. It is a cross between an enormous Wichuraiana, a species climber that aspires to the skies, and a miniature China rose that grows only three or four inches high. Temple Bells still reaches for the sky, but it has the flowers and foliage of the miniature, tiny, tough, glossy foliage with single, delicate white blooms. You can't stop it growing—it is a miniature that has gone haywire. I first saw it dripping down from the top of a wall in Portland, Oregon. It would grow beautifully over a summer-house or a wall. It grows fifteen or twenty feet in a year and flowers once a year on the old wood, that is the second-year wood.

There are other rose firms in the United States, who propagate roses but do not breed them. An enormous number of roses are grown in Texas, but nearly all are for the pre-packed, cheap end of the market.

Some of the things American growers do are not known over here. For instance, when they want to take the foliage off the plants in the fields before lifting in the autumn, to keep them from drying out, they sometimes run sheep in the rose-fields. Sheep do not like rose-leaves at first, but with nothing else to eat they have to learn to like them and they soon get to love the oil in the leaves. I have also seen geese in rose-fields, doing the weeding. There is something comic about geese marching up and down the rows nibbling at the weeds.

One cannot leave out the Edmunds family in the U.S.A. Fred and Wini Edmunds have a compact nursery in Wilsonville in Oregon. Fred is the son of a foreman from Cant's Nurseries in Colchester, who emigrated and started in the U.S.A. before the second world war. Fred and Wini grow a lot of European roses that you would not expect to see there, but they produce them in absolutely perfect quality. They care deeply about their customers and keep closely in touch with them. Fred Edmunds is not a breeder, but a propagator, and he knows every rose that comes out from anywhere. Wini writes to all their customers and knows them by their names and by their addresses—and there are tens of thousands of them—a fascinating business. They probably do not grow more than 250,000 roses, but very profit-ably, and what's more, with wonderful service. They know everything about roses and are absolutely dedicated to them, and to their customers too, who think the world of the Edmunds. It is fantastic to see this couple sitting prosperously in the middle of the American scene, their small firm a midget among the American colossi, with everyone around them growing roses in millions and some of them losing money at it.

The big firms cannot give the attention to their customers that Fred and Wini Edmunds give to theirs. The Edmunds cannot avoid sending out a dud rose plant now and then, as we all do, but when a complaint comes in their apologies are profuse and sincere. Fred does everything to keep his customers happy. All of us larger firms, of course, apologize for the occasional dud plant and replace it, but the fault does not break our hearts as it does his. He will not allow his business to expand, will not grow more roses than he does, because then it would not be the same thing either for him or for his customers. He goes out in the fields in the summer-time and buds roses himself, so that then he can tell the man who buys one that he budded it with his own hands. He drives a tractor about the place, too, and really has a marvellous life because he is doing just what he wants to do. I love one line in his catalogue: 'Don't call and see us on Sundays—your hobby may be roses but mine's fishing.'

There is another wonderful fellow down in Tyler in Texas, called Slick Dean. He is a partner in a firm called A.R.P. Roses. Tyler is the rose centre of Texas, and most of the roses for chain-stores and that kind of business are grown there. So, they have a flourishing rose business, and all of a sudden they find oil in the middle of the nursery. That was sad! Now they can afford to spray oil on the paths to keep the dust down, they have so much of the stuff. In a nearby town they found oil under the bank, so they knocked down the centre of the town to put up oil derricks. Then they found more oil under the supermarket so they knocked that down too. There are derricks now just as close to one another as they can be fitted in. Slick has a couple of magnificent cars, but he prefers to drive round in an old jalopy. He also has what he calls his 'barge', which he runs on a vast man-made lake. When he goes up to his golf-club, which is beside the lake, he drives down to the lakeside in his old jalopy and boards his barge. This barge is really an enormous raft with a platform on top, like a Mississippi steamboat. It is driven by a row of outboards, and there are all home-comforts on board, such as a refrigerator, etc. He just starts up the outboards and away he goes, *putt, putt, putt,* at about two miles an hour in the direction of the golf-club. His neighbours have these things too; and they all get together on one barge or another for 'Slick-Chicks'—a vicious Vodka mixture—and a chat. Slick tails a speedboat along behind his barge, and if he and his wife want to see someone on shore, or aboard another barge, they go off in the speedboat, leaving their barge to continue *putt, putt, putting* along the lake.

Slick is a fantastic fellow. He always wears cowboy boots, without socks. He has his boots hand-made for him with hand-carved letters on them saying 'The Dean of Roses'. Even on formal occasions, when he puts on his tuxedo, he still wears his boots—without socks. No matter where in the world he travels he always wears those boots. One of his joys is the Petroleum Club in Tyler, where one can find all the oil-men living it up, playing housey-housey for astronomical stakes and having their business meetings.

Talking of those cowboy boots, I was sitting beside the President of the American Rose Society, Eldon Lyle, at the American Rose Convention in San Francisco in 1971. We were all in formal wear but Eldon, a good Texan, had on his boots. He did confess to wearing socks, however.

I travel the U.S.A. annually from coast to coast and never fail to be fascinated by it. I travel alone—hard and fast, with as many as twenty flights in a fortnight. That's the way I like it. I reckon I can read the complications of an ABC air timetable better than any travel agent. For preference I fly—by plane for long distances, by helicopter for the hops. In the air I go first class so that I can stretch out my 6ft. 3in. and relax. I devour books and martinis and write speeches. I've taught myself to sleep anywhere because I am one of those people who have to sleep a lot—too fat, I suppose.

One year I went to the U.S.A., from Copenhagen to California, with Niels Poulsen. The clock kept going back and we got fed-up waiting for the cocktail hour—what with the stop-over in Greenland, you can have several breakfasts, play a lot of chess, and drink a lot of beer on that flight. We arrived in Los Angeles at 5 a.m. to be met by Bob Lindquist, but it was 10 o'clock in the evening there, so we had to have just one more party before bed. The tally was four breakfasts, one lunch, no dinner, twenty-six hours without sleep, and quite a hangover.

Most Californian roses are grown around Bakersfield. We drove there, to find a prominent brake-testing station for trucks at the top of a hill. We understood why when we went down—straight down—the other side for what seemed tens of miles. The brakes fade and if they fail all together you just put on your headlights, lean on the horn, and go for the thrilling ride of your life to the bottom.

Bakersfield nurserymen are a happy bunch, given to ribbing each other unmercifully about their crops. They can afford to, as the worst crop I saw was better than any we could grow in Europe. As usual, we checked into a motel. Later in the evening we pleaded tiredness, left our friends in the bar, and retired to our rooms. In pyjamas, Niels remarked that it would be a long time before we were back in California together and it would be a pity to go to bed. I had no desire to change back into my clothes again, so we went back to the bar in our pyjamas—to the delight of our hosts and the surprise of the local populace.

Across the border in Canada lies a different rose world, with a short hot summer, a very cold winter, and no patent protection. At one stage patents were mooted, but, as in many things Canadian, the nurserymen were afraid of the reaction of American big business and the law did not go through. That was a pity, as it has made Canada something of a rose-breeding backwater. The signs are that the climate of opinion is changing, and there is now a Canadian Ornamental Plant Breeders' Foundation, with wide-based support, pressing for protection. I hope it happens, as Canada has a number of very good plantsmen who would quickly push their country to the front, if they had protection to make their plant-breeding an economical proposition.

McGredy roses are handled in Canada by Keith Laver of Pine-haven Nurseries. His town, near Toronto, used to be called Cooksville, but the name was changed to Mississauga. Though I have been going to Canada for years, I have never seen Keith's roses in full bloom. Their season is so late compared to California's, where most of my roses are grown, that to do both in one trip means I cannot see the flowers in the north. I have seen two amateur shows, however, where the quality of bloom was excellent. The Canadians grow many more varieties than the Americans, presumably because of their strong European contacts. The president of their Canadian Rose Society, Milton Cadsby, is a Q.C., which I think must make him unique among rose presidents.

Keith's idea of fun is to fly aeroplanes, build himself a log-cabin for fishing in the far north, where it thaws only for a short season, or hide out in a more luxurious cabin on the Great Lakes, where he builds boats—all kinds of boats. Most people like their greenhouses one storey high, but not Keith. He has one that is at least five times as high. The plants, in trays, go up and round and down on an endless-belt system. He gets more light and earlier crops this way.

In Europe the picture is different, partly because of the smaller scale of things over here. Rose-breeding is still big business, and no firm is bigger than that of the Meillands of France, the breeders of Peace, one of the greatest of roses. Papa Meilland, the grand old man of rose-breeding, died in 1971. There is a hybrid tea named after him, a lovely, well formed, super-fragrant crimson. His son, Francis Meilland, died of cancer in his early forties; he

Kronenbourg

was a marvellous hybridist and just at his peak. Above all others, Francis was the man who fought for patent rights for roses in Europe. He fought and struggled and argued and he prosecuted, and he begged governments to do something, until in the end he got protection for his roses. Patent rights helped him to produce and make money out of a rose called Baccara, a wonderful greenhouse rose and the standard by which all greenhouse roses must now be judged. Baccara and Peace made the Meilland firm. Peace must have earned a million dollars easily and Baccara has earned more since then. There hasn't been anything of the kind from Meilland's since. Now they have a new rose coming this year called Sonia, a salmon hybrid tea for greenhouse forcing, and it is going to be every bit as good as Baccara. They have need of it, to justify the acres and acres of greenhouses they have on valuable land. The Meillands could sell the land now and go off somewhere to live an easy life, but they have their greenhouses and they go on hybridizing and testing, testing, testing, because that is what they want to do.

Alain Meilland, who runs the firm now, is the youngest of rose-breeders, younger than any of the rest of us—the baby, in fact. He is also the smallest, only about 5ft. tall. He is a member of the group of close friends among rose-breeders of which I am happy to be one. I'm 6ft. 3in., Niels Poulsen is 6ft. 3in., Reimer Kordes is 6ft. 5in., and it is one of our delights to have Alain with us, with Jan Spek, who is only a bit taller than Alain. We tell Alain to go and stand with Jan, to make Jan look tall. Perhaps it is being dragged up in greenhouses that has made Niels and Reimer and me so tall, but it has not worked for Jan and Alain.

It has taken the rose-breeders a long time to realize how much they owe to Francis and Alain Meilland and Alain's associate René Royon in their fight to protect patent rights. Alain is proving just as doughty a fighter as his father, and has quickly become a leading character in our rose 'clan'.

I served six years as President of C.I.O.P.O.R.A. (Communauté internationale des Obtenteurs de Plantes ornementales de Reproduction asexuée), the International Organisation of Plant Breeders, with René Royon as secretary; that gave me the opportunity to make one of my most prized friendships. René fights a lot of the Meilland battles for them—and he never gives in. As well as an ability to speak many languages fluently, he is an accomplished magician. He will amuse us by cutting off his finger at the dining-room table. He gives the waiter the bill and money at the end of the meal and the waiter is halfway across the room before he realizes that somehow the money has disappeared from the plate. I have seen his card-tricks turn a formal meeting with the horticultural hierarchy of Hungary in Budapest into a happy, friendly party. The highest compliment I can pay René is to say that he is the one non-rose-breeder completely accepted as one of us.

There are lots of smaller rose-breeders in France who have only a limited amount of international success. My roses are released in France by Paul Pekmez of Strasbourg, who runs N.I.R.P. (Nouveautés internationales de Roses et de Plantes) and is Meilland's biggest competitor; he also represents De Ruiter, Kordes, Tantau, and several of the Americans. Paul is the best-dressed member of our community and looks more as though he belongs on the Stock Exchange than in the slightly grubby world of roses. Looks deceive—he is becoming quite a power in France and makes money for his breeders, which is more than many of those breeders could do for themselves before he came along. I think he sometimes despairs of my own rather casual approach to rose-exploitation. It was for Paul that I named the rose Kronenbourg—the Kronenbourg brewery overshadows his nursery and you never know when you'll be thirsty! We presented the rose at the tercentenary of the brewery after a five-hour luncheon attended by drinkers and dignitaries from all over the world. It is amazing how well roses go with *choucroute* and 'Gewurztraminer' and *foie-gras* and Framboise and Kronenbourg and . . .

There is very little in Spain, except for Pedro Dot, who has been going a long time and is a notable breeder of lavender-blue roses and miniatures. He has another lavender hybrid tea now that looks very good—I have had it on test here and I have seen it in Germany; it should come on the market in the next year or two. Dot has been breeding roses for a long time, but his output is small because he has no protection in Spain and the home market is negligible.

The same problem handicaps Italy. There was a man there called Dominici Aicardi, whom I visited on several occasions. He had lost a lot of his land and his property by backing the wrong side in the second world war and afterwards had only a small nursery in San Remo. He raised Signora, a cerise-pink and salmon hybrid tea rose, one of the very successful roses of my childhood, but now he is dead and I have not heard of his firm for a long time. The full name he gave to his rose was Signora Piero Puricelli.

In Scandinavia, of course, there is Niels Poulsen. It is hard for me to talk dispassionately about Niels because he and I have been close friends for twenty years, and that is why this book is dedicated to him. It was his family that started the polyantha roses, the type that gave rise to the floribundas, the most popular type today. Poulsen's Pearl is typical of that early type (*facing page* 14). Poulsen's was the dominant firm with those roses in the thirties. Else Poulsen, a very famous rose, is still grown after all this time—I saw a big bed of it glowing cherry-pink in the sun outside Cairo airport not very long ago. Else Poulsen, Karen Poulsen, Kirsten Poulsen are all roses named after the girls of the family—I never saw a family with so many beautiful girls. Poulsen's is a big firm, big not only in rose-growing in Scandinavia, but also in breeding fruit trees. Niels' father—'Uncle Svend' to us—bred cherry trees and people laughed at him for taking on something so long-term. Now Niels has magnificent varieties of cherry trees, which he has patented all over Europe, and he is doing very well with them. Trees like that sell by the thousand to single buyers, to a fruit-farmer, for example, and there is a high royalty from them, because the price of a tree is substantial.

The first time I came to Copenhagen, Uncle Svend met me. Although he now denies it vehemently, he took me straight to Tivoli Gardens to see what beer and schnapps would do to the new boy from Ireland. I passed the test. The next hurdle was the approval of Niels and his brother-in-law Knud Sorensen. We took to each other like ducks to water, but for long afterwards they took an unholy delight in pulling my leg. Once when I travelled to Copenhagen by plane, telling my travelling companion next to me what important business commitments I had, I was deeply embarrassed at the airport to be greeted by a gorgeous blonde with a smacking great kiss. Niels and Knud, having put her up to it, were giggling round the corner, but my fellow-traveller gave me a knowing look. Another time I was presented on arrival with a big bouquet of true-blue roses—dyed with Parker's ink! Bob Lindquist had the Poulsen treatment on his first arrival in Denmark after cataloguing his Texan rose as 'tall as a ten-gallon hat, red as a prairie flower, softly scented as a southern belle'. He was presented with a six-foot stem of Chinatown with one tiny bloom on top and a scroll noting that it was 'small as a pint pot, yellow as a rat, and softly scented as a Texas squaw'.

Niels often phones me. He phoned me one rainy day ten years ago, but on this occasion it was different. 'Knud's dead,' he said bluntly. I could not believe it. Some clown had come roaring out of a side road and crashed into his car. It nearly broke my heart. He had been a big half of the Poulsen organization, a live-wire, funny man, and a handsome cuss. That July, Jan Spek, Niels, and I cut a bunch of roses and took them down to Knud's grave. We could not speak. Instead, we wept like babes. We turned and walked to Humlebaek Kro, the local pub, for a beer. Knud would have expected us to do that. We have brought him roses every year since—the hurt is still there.

Humlebaek Kro is a typical Danish village pub and the refuge closest to Niels' home. The locals know us all and join in the general banter. Last year they staged a small exhibit of my newest roses, but had them suitably labelled 'Molly McPoulsen' and 'City of Humlebaek', with Picasso changing to 'Salvador Dali'.

It was Niels who gave me my love of sauna bathing. He has a sauna bath in his basement and we always end the evening there. It is very good for rose-breeders after a long day in the

Arthur Bell

greenhouse or in the fields. I now have a sauna bath at home, where my youngest daughter Maria loves to join me. Bob Lindquist has entertained us in the mineral baths at Soboba Springs near his home. The Finland House Sauna in the Haymarket in London has revived an international gathering of rose-growers before now. I have become something of a connoisseur. My favourite place is the huge Turkish bath near the Reforma in Mexico City. There, the fat and flabby are stretched out on marble slabs in endless rows. Equally fat and flabby masseurs apply their torture before throwing their victims back into the steam-room. In moments of kindness they will fill a bowl of water for your feet and bring you ice-cold beer. Highly civilized. The Japanese bath-houses run the Mexicans a close second, although the probing fingers of their skilled masseuses are not to my liking. I can only giggle at being bathed by a girl— I really think I prefer to have the bath to myself.

I digress. Niels Poulsen has spearheaded the work of Nord-Rose, the Scandinavian nurserymen's organization, which has done much to protect and exploit the rights of plant-breeders. Their secretary, Reider Haggard, controls the issuing of licences and payment of royalties from his Swedish home by the lake at Unnaryd. Every rose tree sold by a Nord-Rose member has to bear their special label. This label is the means of control. If Reider finds any of our varieties being sold without a label, he knows it is illegal. The idea is Meilland's; we use it too, but nowhere is the system better carried out than in Scandinavia.

Time is passing by. Niels' youngest daughter Lise, to whom I stood as godfather, is now a teenager. Niels and Reimer Kordes were groomsmen at my wedding to Maureen. Pernille Poulsen, Birgitte Haggard, and Renate Kordes have been our *au pair* girls. Last year Niels had his fiftieth birthday. He cleared out a huge greenhouse and set up a party—and what a party! Two hundred friends from all over Europe came to congratulate him. I realized with a shock that I knew everyone there, so much have our lives become entwined. Dozens of people had written and some had typed out songs to Niels, which we sang to the accompaniment of a piano-accordion and schnapps. That evening there was inaugurated the Order of the Blue Nose. The rules of this important organization escape me but I do remember that one was never knowingly to refuse a drink. Reimer Kordes, Jan Spek, and I joined Niels on the committee. I do not think we have broken any rules yet.

In Germany there are Kordes and Tantau. Reimer Kordes is my other close friend among rose-breeders. The Kordes family is of a typical German close-knit kind. His Uncle Hermann ruled the family absolutely until the last moment, when he passed the leadership over to his nephew, that is to Reimer Kordes, and now Reimer is the absolute leader. The Kordes live in Sparrieshoop in Holstein, near Elmshorn, north of Hamburg. Reimer has a big nursery—about four million roses a year. Both Reimer and his father Wilhelm have been successful rose-breeders. My memory goes back to Orange Triumph before the war—in 1938, I think— and to the hybrid tea Crimson Glory in 1935, which was a deep velvety crimson and was the acme of red hybrid teas at that time. In recent years Reimer has had Marlena, a dwarf red floribunda, and Peer Gynt, a yellow hybrid tea, among others. The Kordes' commitment to the nursery business is great. They have so much capital tied up in it that they just have to be good. Their large greenhouse department hums with industry, and the constant quest for new garden roses has been somewhat overshadowed by a diligent search for that super greenhouse rose that spells great financial success. They quickly produced the orange Prominent and orange-yellow Esther Ofarim, but I feel that the best is probably still to come. I kid Reimer, who is forty-nine, that he's getting old. It's a sure sign of age when one starts breeding greenhouse-forcing roses—one doesn't have to go out in the rain!

The old Kordes family is interesting. Reimer's father, a man with a forked goatee beard, has retired to a heath outside Hamburg. In the middle of nowhere he has made his own forest and his log-cabin and now and then he disappears out there. He gathers round him all his species crosses, old things that will take years to develop, and there he watches over them. He will not have anything that is not frost-hardy and disease-free. In his forest it is a question of the survival of the fittest for his roses, and if something looks promising he brings it to Reimer to breed. Besides roses, he grows all sorts of things he had no time for when he was young—rhododendrons and so on.

Kordes' brother, Reimer's Uncle Hermann, was about 6ft. 9in. high and weighed over 20 stone, a huge man, but one of the kindliest and the best-liked. He was arrested by the Nazis during the war because he did not sympathize with them, and the whole district, all the farmers and nurserymen, downed tools and would not work until Uncle Hermann was let out again.

Reimer has the capacity to go without sleep—and I have not. Each year we sit until a late hour drinking the good Rhine wine in his home and talking roses. These are great times, but I am always groggy in the morning—and Reimer likes to start at dawn. We are completely frank about our rose-breeding plans. This exchange of information certainly enables us to latch on to a good new breeding line ahead of our competitors. I seem to name a lot of his roses and he mine. Piccadilly and Satchmo were his ideas, Golden Giant and Lili Marlene mine.

The climate and soil in Holstein are wildly different from conditions in Portadown. Roses that have huge flowers with us may have small and insignificant blooms in Germany. It is a chastening experience to see my swans turn into geese after such a short trip. On the other hand, Reimer's plants seem more prone to mildew than some of mine, and often something that looks good in Holstein will be white with the curse in Portadown. A few of my good-looking roses will look good in Holstein and a few of Reimer's are disease-free in Portadown. These are the ones we use for breeding.

As well as a session each year in Germany, Reimer and I always meet in Portadown for a couple of days. I keep a special pair of boots for him, as he's so darned big and our fields are wet most of the time. We walk the rose-seedlings for hours with Ginger McKeown, whom I have already mentioned, as our constant companion. When all the work is over we always end up among large gatherings of Irish or German families and rose-growers. Half of us do not understand the other's language but it does not seem to matter.

Reimer is lucky in that he has two cousins to help him. Werner Kordes runs the nursery and Hermann the office. The bonds between them are strong and good. Werner loves the land, to fish, to hunt, to grow crops. Yet I have probably seen him at his happiest catching tiddlers with the children in a small lake by his home. He lost a leg against the Russians, but it does not slow him down. I must confess it makes his foot a little insensitive on the accelerator—I have the reputation of being, in his passenger seat, the biggest coward of us all.

Reimer's chief rival, Mathias Tantau, lives close by and seems to operate in the same kind of way. He has raised Super Star, which is now the best rose in the world, unquestionably. It is a lovely deep vermilion rose and very unusual in that it is a good greenhouse-forcing rose as well as a garden rose. I cannot think of any other rose that serves both purposes so well. His successes have been mostly in hybrid teas, and he certainly has the knack of producing fragrance with his seedlings. He too has been chasing the greenhouse-forcing market in recent years.

Holland, for all its reputation in horticulture, has not produced many rose-breeders. The best is Gijs De Ruiter. His Christian name should be pronounced something like 'cch-ice', but we cannot manage it, so we call him Charlie—to his disgust. A careful, painstaking hybridist, his biggest success has been Europeana, a rose now grown all over the world and winner of an All-America award. He, like all Dutchmen, has to make every hectare of his land work for him, and his research station is a model of how to get good roses out of a concentrated space. He breeds fewer seedlings than the rest of us, but because he has more time to devote to the testing of each one he probably makes fewer mistakes, and never throws a good one away in error (the rose-breeder's nightmare).

My particular friend in the Netherlands is Jan Spek. He is so old I dare not ask him his age—but he has the energy of a teenager.

The greenhouse-forcing industry is centred in Aalsmeer, the nursery-plant industry is in Boskoop, and never did the twain meet. That was until Jan came along. He burst on the market with an agency for J. & P.'s forcing roses, such as Junior Miss and Zorina, and pushed Niels Poulsen's Nordia to the top of the sales charts. Now he is making Prominent and Esther Ofarim from Kordes the big news of Aalsmeer. He is the one man in Holland who is able to exploit our garden roses too. As he also represents Reimer Kordes and Niels Poulsen he is very much the king-pin of all that goes on in roses in Holland. In a small corner in one of his greenhouses he hybridizes a few miniature roses 'just to keep his hand in'. Niels and I are convinced that he breeds babies only because ordinary roses would be too tall for him! Jan has three sons in the business with him; Hette is the one who handles the roses.

Jan senior has taught me many things, but tolerance is not one of them. Often a group of us will be going through the seedlings at Portadown and I will be trying to encourage one or other of my British licensees to grow a particular variety in his nursery. After having made my sales-pitch I will hear Jan's Scottish-Dutch voice (he learned his English north of the border) muttering: 'I don't think much of *that*.' It always infuriates me, and Jan and I have a good healthy row. Of course he is absolutely right and in my saner moments I thoroughly appreciate and value his candid comments. And are they candid! A compliment from Jan is worth as much to my ego as a gold medal.

Britain is the only other major rose-breeding country in Europe. As our patent or plant variety rights laws date back only to 1964, there are still not many rose-breeders here, but the number is growing. Pat Dickson, who lives only thirty miles away from me, is one of the most important of British rose-breeders. His successes have been mainly in the hybrid tea class. In fact, this year (1971) he has one, two, and three in the new hybrid tea rose audit of the Royal National Rose Society. As I have one, two, and three in the floribundas, we Irish rather dominate the English rose! Grandpa Dickson, a large pale-yellow hybrid tea, has done particularly well in Britain and the U.S.A. Dickson's, incidentally, is a much older company than McGredy's; they have been breeding roses since 1836.

A formidable pair are Alec Cocker in Scotland and Jack Harkness in Hertfordshire. Close friends, they exchange information as Reimer and I do. The net result is that they have quickly been able to make progress in their breeding work. Alec Cocker started, as I did, by taking the best roses from all the rest of us and cross-breeding them. He did it in great volume and it worked well. His best rose to date is Alec's Red, a big, fragrant red hybrid tea. Jack Harkness's approach was rather different. He went for the unusual crosses and this in the long term must be the better bet, as he is doing something different from everybody else and is more likely to produce something distinctly original, to break into a new line. The result is that his roses already look different. His lavender-pink floribunda Escapade is typical. I rate it very highly—one of my three or four favourite roses.

Undoubtedly the best-known English breeder is Edward Le Grice in Norfolk. His deep yellow Allgold must count as one of the greatest roses of the sixties. While none of his other roses has had the same commercial success, many of them are very beautiful. In 1970 his purple lavender News really made news, again the result of an original line of rose-breeding, different from the general run. This emphasizes the advantage of starting off on one's own line. Le Grice achieved something new by using the little-known variety Tuscany as a pollen parent.

In Europe and in the United States, though we are all friends, we do our damnedest to get the better of each other in business, but it is not competition in the same kinds of varieties. Kordes would not want to emulate my strain of breeding, he would not want his roses to look like mine, nor would Meilland want his to look like mine or Kordes'. Either of them might take one of my roses to incorporate it into his hybridizing programme, but by the time he had results from it I would be three or four rose-generations farther on.

Kordes and Poulsen may be competitors, but they sell their

roses in Britain through me. Meilland used to sell through Wheatcroft, but now sells through Odell. Tantau sells through Wheatcroft, and Gregory handles many of De Ruiter's varieties. I do not sell directly in France, but through an agent, so Meilland and I can be good friends. Meilland does not hammer at me: he hammers at Odell in England to try to make him produce a better catalogue and more effective selling methods than mine.

Outside Europe and the U.S.A. there is little rose-breeding of any importance. Japan is obviously going to be a competitor in the future—when I was last there six years ago they were just beginning to get started. Teams of hybridists were beginning to breed roses on a grand scale, but it is too early yet to say how they will turn out.

Although it has no patent laws and no breeders of note, New Zealand boasts a considerable market because roses grow so very well there. My roses are handled by Phil Gardner of Avenue Nurseries, Levin. Small in stature, he has some odd hobbies—such as training people to climb the Himalayas or to cross the Antarctic. For me his most notable achievement was a series of back somersaults in real professional fashion across the length of a rather staid bar in Levin. He also works, with deep application; I cannot think of many people who could take an external botany degree while running a nursery, but Phil did. He and his wife Georgie have good eyes for a rose. They picked out Tiki, which has proved to be one of my most successful roses in New Zealand. I cannot repeat often enough that nowhere in the world do roses grow as well as they do in New Zealand.

One of the very great ornamental shrub nurseries of the world is to be found in North Island. The Davies family run a superb nursery, called Duncan & Davies, in New Plymouth. Not only can they grow a wide range of plants, from *Leptospermums* to the Norfolk Island pine, that cannot survive in our climate, but they can also grow many of the South African *Proteas*. One gets used to seeing outstanding nurseries in the northern hemisphere, but D. & D. is a real pearl 'down under'.

In our permissive and casual age the obvious respect and adoration of the Davies children for their father Trevor make a deep impression. Bob and Ellie Lindquist and I spent an hilariously happy day with the family a few years back. If you are moving around the world like a madman, as I often am, a relaxed day with happy people such as they are is a tonic.

When I am in New Zealand I try to find time for a week-end at Rotorua. On one visit Mayor Linton put on a special concert for me because I had said I would like to hear Maori music. The singers were led by an old woman called Guide Kiri, whose seventieth birthday it chanced to be. She whispered in my ear that I should come on afterwards to a real Maori party at the Whakarewarewa—that was the Maori village. So after Phil Gardner and I had finished dinner with the mayor, we went and drank beer with Kiri and the Maoris. They are splendid, happy people who are apt to break out spontaneously into fun and games, and they dance and sing as though they loved to do nothing better. I remember seeing a number of Maoris having a birthday party in a restaurant; suddenly, impromptu, they jumped up and burst into song and dance. The Maoris produce good singers and very fine choirs. I called a rose Pania, after a maiden of Maori folk-lore, and the world-famous St. Joseph's Maori Girls' Choir gave me a tape of a song they sang specially for me because I had called a rose by a Maori name. That is a treasured possession —collecting music tapes and records is my best-loved hobby.

Equally treasured is the memory of a day when Phil and I were smuggled into the meeting-house at the *pa* or fortified village at Whakarewarewa. Sitting quietly in a corner, the only two *pakehas*, or Europeans, in the hall, we watched an official delegation from western Samoa greet their Maori neighbours in a manner unchanged through hundreds of years. The copious exchange of gifts and flowers and jewellery, the swaying, singing dancers with graceful hands, the *hakas* and *nuaos*, their peculiar chants of war or welcome, the downright simple pleasure of unabashed affection for each other, left a lasting impression on us.

We went bathing with the Maoris too. Kiri invited us to come

Jan Spek

up one morning to the *pa* where the hot springs are. There they have a pool with hot water coming out of the ground through a pipe into one end of the pool and just flowing away at the other end, so that the water is always fresh. There were men and women and children all bathing together, so we just took everything off and went in.

That reminds me too of a bath I took in Japan, where it is the usual thing to bath before dinner. I was shown to a bathroom and given a kimono to wear when I came out again. Unfortunately Japanese houses are not made for people of my size and weight, and when I stepped on the bathroom floor I went straight through it!

In Australia, my agent is Roy Zielke, who runs the Langbecker Nurseries at Bundaberg, Queensland. Now Bundaberg is hot and sticky, there is no real winter there, and many of the Australian rose hierarchy who live in the south of the continent think of Queensland as a place with nothing more than small tropical roses and frost-tender plants. I heard this a lot and in my sweet Irish way took no notice; for the Queenslanders were prepared to pay royalties on my roses when the rest of the continent had nothing to offer. Roy and his team work very hard to represent me, and he and I became pals very quickly. I enjoy the slightly whacky manner of the Queenslanders, which sets them apart—rather in the way the Irish are different from the English.

My picture, of course, gets in their local paper, and I am instantly known. The laundryman stops me in the street, saying he has seen my picture: he supposes that I must be travelling fast and if he could do some quick laundry or dry-cleaning for me, he would like to help. This is typical.

Bundaberg is sugar-cane country. Cane-cutting makes tough men—ten years ago, the local hostelry used to be filled with men of iron drinking gallons of beer. Much of the cutting is mechanized now. In the hotel I was given a clean room with mosquito nets over twin-beds. As the hotel-keeper's wife showed me the room she said: 'I hope you'll be comfortable, Mr. McGredy, and we'll try not to put anyone in with you.' If anyone in the bar drank too much beer or 'Red Ned' and could not make it home, he would have had the other bed! Fortunately it did not happen. There was a communal wash-room with toilets, showers, and shaving-plugs all together. You may start off knowing nobody, but by the time you get down to breakfast you know all the men, at least. The tea trolley comes round the hotel corridors at 6 a.m. Anyone who has been in hospital knows how impossible it is to sleep through that. Just as I dozed off again up went the cry 'Laundry!' as my street friend came the rounds looking for trade. When the morning paper came through the open sky-light above the bedroom door and landed on my belly I gave up and got up for my steak and egg breakfast. New hotels, of course, are springing up now, but the frontier atmosphere is still there.

As I have said, the bloom quality of roses is poor in all that heat, but the plants grow beautifully. Half an hour's flying-time away, in Brisbane, the same varieties bloom considerably better.

My favourite rose organization of Australia is the Queensland Rose Society, whose principal is Hugh Graham. He leads a really happy, fun-loving bunch of rose-growers. Most amateur rose-meetings I have been at tend to be formal, but not the meetings in Queensland. Everybody derives obvious enjoyment out of showing roses and discussing roses, or in contending and debating with the speaker of the evening. The evening ends, as it always does in Australia, with the ladies at one end of the room, the men at the other, and beer. The Queenslanders made me an honorary member of their rose society and so I am one of them.

One day I shall go farther south, to Melbourne or Adelaide, where I hear that Australian roses grow to the best effect.

5. THE NAMING OF ROSES

A new rose, after its long evolution and various trials, is ready to go on the market, ready to take its place among all those that have gone before in garden, park, or greenhouse. Until this time this new rose has been known to the public only by numbers relating to plants growing in trial-grounds in various countries. Now it has come through the trials and has perhaps won an award or two, and it is judged worthy to have a place in the breeder's catalogue. It needs a name or title by which it will in future be known.

The choosing of names should be no automatic or simple business. One would suppose that the name should be easy to understand and to pronounce, that it should in some way represent or conjure up a picture of the rose to which it is applied, that it should be easy to remember, and finally, if at all possible, that it should be spelled in the same way and be pronounceable in any language, or at least in many languages.

It would be idle to assert that all these desirable qualities are achieved in the naming of more than a very few roses. A moment's examination of books on roses and of rose-growers' catalogues will show numerous names that exhibit a total disregard of most or even of all the requirements suggested above. Many other considerations seem to apply, and some of these are not especially relevant to roses in general or in particular.

Rose names fall into four categories:

1. Commemorative or complimentary
2. Sentimental
3. Descriptive or connotative
4. Commercial

Under the heading of commemorative or complimentary names comes a vast quantity of roses named after people, and mostly after women; some of these names are in sound and appearance wildly at variance with the conception of a rose. Mrs. A. R. Barraclough, Percy Izzard, Florence Haswell Veitch, Edith Nellie Perkins, and the famous Dorothy Perkins are names of this kind, names not in themselves attractive but applied for good reasons. For example, the Perkins roses commemorated members of the Perkins family of Jackson & Perkins, while Mrs. Barraclough was the wife of the president of the Royal National Rose Society at that time and her name would therefore have been familiar to the many rose gardeners who were members.

That such names are good names for roses is a matter of opinion, but that some such names are in themselves ugly cannot be doubted. Mrs. Wemyss Quin, Fred Loads, Edith Nellie Perkins, E. J. Ludding are examples of names that do not suggest the poetic qualities of the rose. Germanic names sometimes appear especially unpoetic, at least in English- and French-speaking countries. It is difficult to picture roses corresponding to the names of Frau Karl Druschki (called Snow Queen in English) or of Parkdirektor Riggers and Klaus Störtebeker, both from Kordes, or of Florida von Scharbeutz and Bischofstadt Paderborn. Schneewittchen is charming in meaning (Snow White), but it is not a handsome word; it is Kordes' name for the rose known in English as Iceberg. That is not to say that Germany cannot produce more appropriate and more attractive names, but it does seem easier in the Romance languages to find names that are fine-sounding and evocative. Pedro Dot's penchant for Spanish noble titles brought some richly connotative and resounding rose names, such as Duquesa de Penaranda and Condesa de Sastago, which at least suggest something fine and colourful. One cannot help wondering if Countess of Gosford and City of Leeds appear as romantic to a Spaniard.

Some names, English or foreign, sound absurd in themselves. President Cochet-Cochet is inexplicably comic, but this name was given to a rose in 1937 by the breeder Mallerin. Gooiland

City of Leeds

Glory of 1925, by Van Rossem, is another example of unfortunate naming.

Personal names, innocuous in themselves, lend themselves to ridiculous verbal situations, usually unconscious rather than intentional, such as one may hear in conversations between rose-enthusiasts. Not many ladies would enthuse about their eponymous roses being described as 'good bedders', nor might Mrs. Franklin Roosevelt altogether have approved her description in a rose book as 'an exceptionally beautiful sport'. Another danger appears in the crossing of roses that have personal names. In my own catalogue, for example, you will find the astounding information that Elizabeth of Glamis and Casanova are the parents of Courvoisier!

The problems of foreigners in pronouncing English words are not made any easier by many of the names applied to roses. After the usual struggle with vowel conjunctions such as 'ough' in 'cough', 'rough', bough', etc., the foreigner will be in total doubt what to do about such names as Mrs. A. R. Barraclough, Mrs. Charles Lamplough, and so on, problems in which he will be joined by many Englishmen. Elizabeth of Glamis puzzles probably as many rose-enthusiasts in English as in any other language—there are still plenty of Englishmen who think of the Queen Mother as 'Elizabeth of Glammiss', and this is how foreigners inevitably attempt to pronounce this name. Even ordinary words applied as names of roses are not exempt from such problems. Mischief is clear enough to any Englishman, and a Frenchman would pronounce it in much the same way, lengthening the vowels a little, so that it becomes more like 'Mees Sheef'; but an Italian would make it 'Meeskee-eff'. The invention of names that will look the same and be pronounced the same in any language is very difficult indeed, and it has occupied the attention of many large international industrial firms in fields other than roses. The name of Kodak was deliberately contrived to answer this problem, and it has been successful (except in pronunciation—on the Continent it is liable to become 'Koddak'), but it is in itself a word that means nothing and evokes

G

nothing other than what has been imported into it by the many products and services of the company.

Perhaps in an attempt to overcome the problems some rose-growers have adopted names of famous people, as both a compliment and a safeguard, but the result is usually a rose-name that dates rather rapidly. One can expect that roses named after Edith Cavell—and there are at least two—would date from the first world war, and it is equally probable that Don Bradman would be about 1930. Charmaine obviously belongs to about 1925, and Soraya must come from the late 1950s, when that beautiful but unfortunate queen was in the news.

The dividing line between names that are commemorative and those that are complimentary or sentimental is slight. The various names of members of the families of rose-breeders may be said to be of this second category—such names as Mrs. Sam McGredy, Molly McGredy, Paddy McGredy, Karen Poulsen, and Kirsten Poulsen belong here. The same criticisms apply to personal names in this category as to those of the commemorative kind. What should be noticed, however, is that the tendency to use formal names, such as Mrs. A. R. Barraclough, is now less emphatic. Informal versions of personal names seem to consort better with a rose, especially when the names are diminutives, as Molly McGredy and Paddy McGredy.

Meilland wanted his beautiful new rose to be called Mme A. Meilland, after his wife; it was a stroke of genius on the part of the American grower, at that time, to call it Peace. It has also acquired the names Gioia and Gloria Dei.

The naming of Lili Marlene was a memorable and happy occasion. Kordes had a new red rose at a time when Pat Dickson and I were visiting him. One evening Pat and I joined the Kordes family in their living-room, where we all sat round a table on which was a huge bowl of a kind of punch or cup made with Rhine wine, champagne, and peaches. Each of us was supplied with a big stein, which we dipped into the bowl every time we wanted replenishment. It wasn't long before we were all singing loudly and banging our mugs on the table, and it was inevitable that we should sing the song 'Lili Marlene'. I suggested that the new rose should be called by this name, and this was put to the meeting and agreed there and then. That is as good a way of christening a rose as any!

Other complimentary or sentimental names selected by rose-breeders are those of their friends or of persons admired, as for instance Jan Spek, which I chose for a very successful rose named for one of my best friends, and Esther Ofarim, for a singer whose style Kordes likes. Alec Rose, who sailed alone round the world, seemed to me an obvious choice, because of his name, but it was I who asked him first. Hector Deane was the doctor who took out my tonsils, and Adair Roche was the architect who designed my house on the hill overlooking the nursery. Margot Fonteyn is a name I chose as commemorative, complimentary, and sentimental all at once for this petite, beautiful, and inspired ballet dancer. The name of Ginger Rogers, a very different kind of dancer, and actress, was used for similar reasons. Lady Seton is the married name of Julia Clements, who is well known as a lecturer and exponent of floral arrangement. I admire Violet Carson for her acting as Ena Sharples in *Coronation Street* and that was sufficient excuse for me to name a rose after her. We both insisted that it should *not* be Ena Sharples. Uncle Walter is named for Walter Johnston, who was mainly responsible for keeping the McGredy nursery in being during the twenty years of my minority.

Pania reminds me of pleasant times in New Zealand—it is, as I have already mentioned, the name of a Maori maiden famous in folk-lore. The South African desert gave me Kalahari. Kerry-man comes from the fact that out of all of Ireland the county of Kerry is the part Maureen and I like best to visit, and with this one name I honoured at a stroke the kind and charming people of that county and also my friend Dan Nolan, who is the editor of the newspaper called the *Kerryman*. Rose of Tralee I named both for the song and for the festival that has been held annually at Tralee for some years now; I find it amazing that no rose-breeder before me had thought of using this name. City of

Belfast reminds any rose-enthusiast of the beautiful trial-grounds and rose-garden in my native Ireland, and reminds me of the honour I had to be concerned in its foundation. It is also a compliment to Belfast Parks Director, Reg Wesley. One of the best flower-shows in the North of England is in the City of Leeds—hence their rose.

Descriptive names may be apt, witty, or evocative. They should, of course, bear some relation to the qualities of the rose concerned—they should refer to its colour, to its manner of blooming, to the shape of the bloom or the habit of the plant, or to its fragrance, or some other characteristic. The very name Fragrance could be described as witty in the classical sense of the word if only because no one had thought of applying it to a rose before 1924. Heaven Scent is also a witty name for a rose with a remarkable fragrance, and I would also class as witty such names as Mallerin's Feu d'Artifice, Poulsen's Chinatown, Von Abrams' Golden Slippers, Dickson's Sunstar, Meilland's Allegro and Tzigane, and my own Bridal Robe and Picasso. Such names suggest one or more qualities implicit in one word. Perhaps I might add Piccadilly, which I chose for the bright lights, and Mischief, a word that seems to me appropriate and enchanting without my really being able to say why. Mischief came about in an amusing way. I was arranging a display of a new rose at the Summer Rose Show of the Royal National Rose Society, watched by the president of the society, Major-General R. F. B. Naylor. He said: 'Why not call that rose Mischief?' and I adopted the idea at once. It was only later that I discovered that it was the name of his dog!

This reminds me of another dog story. At the nursery we are always receiving letters from people who have suggestions about the naming of roses. One such letter asked us to give a rose the name 'Inter'. Curious about this, we wrote to ask why? Back came a letter saying that Inter was a dog that had recently died. It had belonged to a vicar who was very fond of it and the writer thought that it would be a nice thing for the vicar if a rose were named 'Inter' in memory of the dog. We were still puzzled, so we asked, why 'Inter', to be told a day or two later that 'Inter' was short for 'Interdenominational'. There we left it.

More purely descriptive are such names as my Orangeade, De Ruiter's Orange Sensation, and Kordes' Orange Triumph; they reflect our pleasure in breeding successful orange-coloured roses. Flamenco is a little more oblique, but gives an idea of what kind of rose to expect. Fragrant Cloud, from Tantau, is apt for a rose sweetly fragrant and free-flowering—in German it is Duftwolke and in French Nuage parfumée, both literal translations.

Translations of rose names are not very common and not always exact. Kordes' Independence is in the original German Sondermeldung, which means 'special report'; it is also called Geranium and Reina Elisenda. My Picasso, an example of an oblique name for a rose, is recognizable throughout the world, with little danger of miscomprehension or mispronunciation. I chose it, with permission, for the first of a series of roses that I call 'hand-painted'. Poulsen's Snowline, emerging as one of the best roses of the seventies, describes a rose that is white with a little of the pink that the rising or setting sun casts on snow.

Super Star suggests something superlative, as this rose is. Tantau had wanted to call it Ilse Tantau, for his wife, but was dissuaded by Gene Boerner, who chose Super Star. This was incautious, or forgetful of the existence of the Star Rose Company of Pennsylvania—so for American use only Super Star became Tropicana.

A rose that gave me an amusing time because of the name I chose for it was Garvey, which I brought out in 1960. It was a rose beginning as a peach pink, deepening in colour towards a rich salmon as it opened. I wanted to honour the excellent sherry made by the Garvey Sociedad Anonime, and my good Irish friend and Garvey agent, Jack McCabe.

The directors were so pleased with this they invested me with the Insignia of the Honorary Capataz of the Bodegas of San Patricio, that is to say they made me an honorary foreman, a title they regard as one of great distinction. At the same time they also conferred the honour on Jack McCabe and Dr. Richard

Hayward, the Irish author. I was delighted—but I was astonished when they added that I was free to travel anywhere in Spain at Garvey's expense. I thought they must be joking, but no, they were very serious. I said that was splendid, that I was coming to Spain in the spring to the Madrid trials-gardens, and I would like to have a car, but they need not pay my hotel bills. Certainly, they said, it shall be done. I have never encountered greater courtesy and generosity.

Niels Poulsen and Jan Spek and I have long made it our custom to meet once a year at one important show or another, which we have selected in turn. I rang up Niels in Denmark and Jan in Holland and told them that we would be going to Madrid this year, and explained why. They could not believe it, but when we arrived at the airport at Madrid, there to meet us, by courtesy of Garvey, was an English-speaking chauffeur, Mike, with a large American Plymouth car. He brought us everywhere we wanted to go throughout our stay. In the hotel I was received with honour: 'Ah, Mr. McGredy, you are the honorary *capataz*. We are very pleased to see you.' There were bottles of sherry in our rooms—indeed, it seemed to us that there were bottles of sherry everywhere we went. I never saw so much sherry and I certainly never drank so much of it in so short a time.

As usual, all nationalities of rose-breeders and journalists had gathered for the opening of the Madrid show. The city had laid on a coach to take them for an outing to Segovia, which has a famous restaurant. Niels, Jan, and I went in our Plymouth, and we would dash on, overtaking the coach, to stop at the next bar, where we would sit and drink our sherry and watch the coach go by. We were like small boys wanting to make the rest of the gang jealous. And so we leap-frogged all the way into Segovia.

In Madrid we were given a magnificent champagne reception. We found it very slow in starting, and evidently nothing much was going to happen until the mayor arrived, which he did late in the evening. Then the fun began as though to a starting-gun. With little Jan in the middle and Niels and I at his side, we were pressed up against the bar unable to move and not wanting to.

We were stuck to that bar, drinking champagne and passing glasses and bottles of it over our shoulders to those milling behind us. 'Don't move,' we laughed to each other, 'for God's sake don't move.' We struck up a friendship with a man and his wife in this seething throng. The man was something to do with the city of Madrid, and he was here with his wife and his grandmother and I don't know who else. We agreed to go out for the evening together and they would show us some of the nightspots. Then, unfortunately, Niels dropped the most resounding of clangers. We were going off to freshen up and Niels insisted on kissing the Spaniard's wife goodbye. Now nobody in Northern Ireland, or in our international rose circle for that matter, would mind in the least if a man gave his friend's wife, in public, a friendly kiss, but it is not done in Spain, and Niels' effort seemed to change the whole tone of the party. Suddenly no one wanted to know us any more and the evening broke up in what seemed to us an inexplicable chill.

When we left in the morning Niels and Jan watched from a distance as I went to pay my bill at the hotel desk. They still did not believe that it could be true about Garvey and wanted to see what would happen, half-expecting that I would be given a massive account for everything we had had. But no—the hotel would not let me pay for anything. I was the honorary *capataz* of Garvey and that was that. Blessed be the name of Garvey and may their excellent sherry long flourish!

The basis of the practice of using sponsored names for roses is simply that a good rose goes far and wide over many countries and carries the name of the sponsor with it. It is both good advertising and good public relations. It is part of the creed of advertising and publicity that the more often the name of a company or of its product is mentioned or printed, the better it is for that company and for the sales of the product, and if the name occurs in a pleasant connotation, that is all to the good. Almost every rose-breeder has at some time or other agreed to give roses commercial names in return for payment, in cash or kind, and I have no doubt that those who have not done it would like to. I believe I have been more successful in this field than perhaps anyone else.

One of my earliest successes was the *Daily Sketch* rose, which was publicized by that newspaper from 1961 onwards. Evelyn Fison was named in 1962 for the wife of the managing director of the Fison fertilizer company; the company used the rose in colourful beds around its offices in the large converted hotel it has at Felixstowe, and also at its branches, and sent plants to its customers in many places. Courvoisier was named in 1969 for the brandy, and John Church in 1964 for the manufacturer of shirts, while Irish Mist was for the liqueur whiskey made in Ireland at Tullamore. The National Trust rose of 1970 was advertised through the Trust's mailing list and was sold at many of the National Trust properties—they got 20 pence of the price of 50 pence and we got 30 pence. Arthur Bell carries the name of a famous Scotch whisky, and the colour too, for it is a rose of clear yellow tint. My reward for this was innumerable cases of whisky.

The rose Silent Night was named for a mattress company, who paid me £2,000 for the privilege, and it is appropriate that this rose is accurately described as 'an ideal bedder'. Not all names are as apt to the product, and John Church and Marie-Elizabeth perhaps do not at once recall shirts and sardines respectively. The name 'Mullard', however, does connote electricity and electronics everywhere in the world and the word 'jubilee' emphasizes the length of time the firm has been in existence. The company paid a fee of £10,000 to have a rose called Mullard Jubilee. That may seem a very high price, but it is for a rose that is quite out of the ordinary, a rose of very fine quality that is going to be prominent in the market for the next ten years at least. Mullard Jubilee has already won high honours, and in particular it has won the top American award, a feat that has not been achieved by any British hybrid tea rose since 1947. Mullard Jubilee will be carrying the name of Mullard in nearly all countries of the globe for many years to come.

My latest ventures into the field of sponsored roses are one for Yellow Pages, the Thomson 'phone guide, and another for

Coventry Cathedral; for the latter I have bred a rose, to be called Coventry Cathedral, that will be sold during their tenth anniversary as a money-raiser for the cathedral.

There is always likely to be criticism of sponsoring and indeed some curious names have been applied to roses through sponsorship. Mullard Jubilee may not be ideal, but 'Jubilee' is a name that might well have been applied to a rose in the normal way. Courvoisier is a name that has something to say in colour, flavour, and intoxication that a rose may, with little imagination, represent—though it will not smell like brandy! In America Chrysler Imperial is a name with resemblances in motivation to Mullard Jubilee—'Imperial' might easily have been chosen for a rose. Lammerts, who bred this rose, was given a free Chrysler car, which is rather as though Rolls-Royce might sponsor a rose and give the breeder a free Rolls. Gail Borden was named for the American dairy firm. Perhaps the least appropriate, in image at least, among sponsored names is First Federal Savings, for an American bank.

Among the most outstanding and touching circumstances concerning the sponsored naming of roses is the story of Bobbie Lucas. I received a letter from an Englishman called Altson who wanted to know if it was possible for a rose to be named after a lady of his acquaintance. Well, quite a lot of letters like that come into the office, and I send details to all such correspondents. I answered in the usual way, told him the cost, and said that I could let him have a list of the reference numbers of McGredy roses that were then growing in trial-grounds near his home, from which he would be able to choose. I did not think that anything more would come of this, but back came the reply from Mr. Altson saying 'Yes, indeed, very interested', and please would I let him have the numbers. That was that for a time, until I heard from a solicitor saying that as Mr. Altson was very old and infirm he did not expect that I would hear any more of the matter. About two years later a letter came from another solicitor telling me that Altson had died and had left £5,000 for a rose to be called The Pretty Bobbie Lucas Rose. The background

97

of this was that Altson, who had been an artist, and a good one too, after the death of his wife had brought a woman called Bobbie Lucas into his house to care for him in his old age. In fact, it turned out that he more often had to take care of her, and she died before he did; but he had grown fond of Bobbie Lucas, and he had now left money to have a rose named after her and to have a bed of it planted outside a hospital in Australia to which he or she owed some acknowledgement. I provided half a dozen trials numbers for the solicitor, Mr. Perkins, to choose a rose, explaining that at that stage I could not say which rose would turn out to be the best. He looked at the roses and made his choice purely on the basis of personal preference. I had suggested that the name The Pretty Bobbie Lucas Rose was too long, and he agreed to shorten it to Bobbie Lucas. In due course the Bobbie Lucas rose was put on the market and I arranged for a bed of it to be planted in the grounds of the hospital in Australia.

Bobbie Lucas, however, though it was the Rose of the Year for 1967, proved not to be the best of the group of roses I had submitted, and this year (1971) is the last year it will appear in my catalogue. Among others in the group were roses later called Banbridge, Santa Fé, and Irish Mist, and the last of these proved to be by far the best. Bobbie Lucas roses, however, with their full, deep salmon-orange blooms, are likely to adorn private gardens for a long time to come.

Another aspect of naming concerns not individual varieties of roses, but the groups into which they may be classified, such names as hybrid perpetual, hybrid tea, floribunda, and the American grandiflora. There is now an international committee for the nomenclature of plants, which meets every four or five years in one country or another. The committee is, however, rather a scientific body than a commercial one, and it tends to choose names, or to construct names, that have a botanical or Latin basis. In doing this they take little or no account of sales values and produce names with Latin roots that are foreign to the language of the country.

There is discussion at present concerning a name for the new type of rose represented by Marlena, Jan Spek, and Picasso. These are dwarf, bushy roses and there are proposals that they should be called 'compacta'. I would prefer the English 'cushion roses' as more immediately comprehensible and saleable. But the committee takes little notice of commercial needs or of the desires of the people who breed the plants submitted to them for nomenclature. I am and am always likely to be at war with this body of gentlemen.

6. MARKETING ROSES

Marketing is a complex operation that begins long before a new variety is ready to be launched. It includes the sending of roses to trial-grounds throughout the world (and in my case also to the three thousand members of the McGredy Better Roses Club), the exhibition of roses at flower-shows and festivals, advertising, the preparation and dispatch of catalogues, public-relations operations, the building up of stocks to meet estimated demand, the licensing of propagators, and so on down to methods of packaging and dispatch.

The first thing to be considered in this story is the change in the market since about 1965. Mail-order was, and had been as long as anyone could remember, the kingpost of the rose business and innumerable firms in Europe and America flourished in mail-order, selling roses in enormous quantities—I have already commented on the vast sales of Jackson & Perkins, which reached a level of many millions of plants every year. The prosperity of the mail-order business and the ease of selling by this method were euphoric, and none of us was prepared for what happened. There was a sudden fall in mail-order sales, which went on dropping for the next five or six years and are only now beginning to show signs of levelling off. America has perhaps reached stability already, but Britain tends to follow on the American pattern, perhaps a year or two behind. In the process many firms of rose-growers went to the wall, both in America and in Europe, and others found their business considerably reduced and their profits disappearing. Some of the smaller firms closed down, some went bankrupt, some found themselves being bought out by larger companies. In all this welter the one part of the rose business that

remained comparatively stable was that of rose-breeding, and if
I had not been a breeder as well as a propagator I might have been
a very unhappy rose-man. The demand for new roses goes on,
and this part of the business is not one that is easily taken over,
for any rose-breeding operation rests basically on the flair of one
man; if that man is not willing to be taken over, there is little to
buy other than greenhouses, fields, and a breeding-stock.

The increasing costs of the rose business, in postage, carriage,
wages, and so on, indicate a future different in many respects from
the past. It seems to me that mail-order in the rose industry is
bound to become one of super-quality at consonant high prices,
and that is the direction I shall take. I might have said that
McGredy's would become the Rolls-Royce of rose-breeders if
recent events had not made that analogy somewhat ambivalent.

The fall in mail-order sales left practically every rose-grower
unprepared, with thousands of unsold roses at the end of the
season. The more optimistic or hopeful the grower had been,
the larger was the quantity of unsold roses left on his hands. It
was natural that the best plants were the ones that were sold first
and that those left behind included many that were second-best.
In a normal year a rose-grower would burn his surplus, so that
it never came on the market, but in the new conditions, with falling sales and huge surpluses, he cut the price and sold as many
plants as he could to wholesale buyers, who pre-packed them and
sent them out to supermarkets and department stores. All rose-
growers took part in this, though we were cutting off our noses
to spite our faces, and working in a market that had no firm
foundation for the future. As soon as stability is achieved in the
normal markets for roses, growers will propagate only the number
of plants they reasonably think they can sell and there will be no
sizeable surplus to dispose of to the cheaper market. That market
will then disappear for lack of supplies, unless some rose-
propagator or other decides that there may be a living in growing
lesser-quality plants to keep the cheaper end of the trade supplied.

That the plants sold in this way are second-class cannot be
doubted, and it would be foolish of the buyer to suppose that he

can get for 15 pence in a supermarket or multiple store the same quality of plant as he would buy from me or from another reputable nursery for 35 pence or 60 pence. The British Standard for rose plants imposes a requirement that a first-quality plant must have not less than two good stems of stated thickness. Not many of the pre-packs can meet this requirement, and if they did the plants would not fit so neatly into the packs as in fact they do. McGredy plants are invariably better than the British Standard, and have three or four, and sometimes more, good stems when they leave my nursery ready for planting. This is the kind of business I want to pursue. I want McGredy's to be known for the high quality of its plants, and I have no intention of chasing the cheap end of the business.

The packaging of roses is a matter of considerable importance. The ideal in the sale of a rose is to take it out of the ground in the nursery and to replant it on its new site in a matter of days. The worst one can do with a rose is to pack it in cardboard or paper, for the longer it remains in such a pack the more the board and paper will suck the moisture out of the plant and shrivel it up. We pack our roses in plastic-coated bags in order to retain the moisture. Pre-pack roses are usually sold in a polythene pack with a strip of card on which details and usually a picture of the rose are printed. This is a good pack if the card is not too absorptive, and if the rose is not held too long—not more than three weeks—and is not kept at too high a temperature. If such packs could be kept in a cooler of some kind at about 40 degrees F. it would be ideal, but what happens is that the pack goes on the counter in a shop maintained at 60 or 70 degrees. In these conditions the pack becomes a miniature greenhouse and the plant starts to grow and so to weaken itself, since it is drawing on its diminishing reserves. Plants packed in containers filled with soil or compost, as sold in many garden-centres, stand up to travel a lot better, for they can, and indeed should, be replanted with the earth intact.

I have two hundred thousand customers in the British Isles and many more in other countries. Then there are also the rose-propagating firms, who take McGredy roses on licence. Such firms do not necessarily propagate on to the same understocks as I and other breeders do and the quality of the plant is not under our control. Nevertheless one can depend on the well known propagators, of whom Mattock is an example, giving satisfactory quality to their customers. Since the plant patents act came on to the statute book propagators have had to pay commissions to the breeder for every rose of his that they sell.

Another avenue I am following is the creation of a chain of franchised dealers, each of whom will be the only dealer in his area allowed to sell McGredy roses. Their plants will be of high quality, of course, carrying the McGredy name, and in general the franchised dealer will be the owner of a garden-centre; the local public can come there for McGredy roses if they do not want to send for them from me directly.

The confusing change in the structure of the mail-order market prompted me to brief two market-research firms to investigate that market and to give me a picture of the changes that had occurred in the rose-buying public and the causes for those changes. I knew well enough what the market had been in my father's day and before the war. Then the backbone of the business had been the upper middle-class, the owners of large houses and large gardens who employed one or more gardeners. They ordered roses lavishly and set them thickly in the ground, making them bloom madly by feeding them with quantities of manure and fertilizer. In three or four years the plants expired from exhaustion, after a short but colourful life, and then our customers of that day simply re-ordered. It was clear from this that a nurseryman might expect a renewal of orders every three or four years.

The two market-researches were very different in method. The first took a sample covering 2,900 people classified into the usual AB, C1, C2 and DE classes—that is to say, managerial and administrative, supervisory and clerical, skilled manual labourers, and semi-skilled or unskilled men. The result of this enquiry was the discovery that McGredy's customers included a high proportion of middle-aged and middle-class people, with middle-sized rather than large gardens; but, and this was important, there was also a large number of working-class people with small gardens who were rose-enthusiasts and bought plants in quantities from six to a dozen. It was a number of the people in this last group who deemed the image of Sam McGredy in a business suit inappropriate for a rose-breeder—they would have preferred to see me in overalls or baggy old trousers and a cardigan.

The second research was concerned with a much smaller number of people, but they were carefully selected from among the customers of the nursery and they were interviewed much more thoroughly. These subjects were classified as 1966 customers who had re-ordered in 1967 and in 1968, 1966 customers who had re-ordered in *either* 1967 or 1968, and customers who had bought in 1966 and had not re-ordered. The result of the survey was clear enough, confirming what we already knew rather than revealing new information. Nearly all the people who bought roses did so because they wanted hardy and vigorous plants that would blossom for a long period each year with no more than a small amount of attention. Each member of the groups bought and continued to buy until he thought he had a full garden, and then ceased, not to begin again until plants died and left gaps. The question was what was defined as a full garden. While gardeners with mixed gardens valued their flower-beds and the lawns in which they were set, the true rose-enthusiast was likely to create new beds by digging up his lawn.

Many people considered that large local nurseries were the best source of plants, because customers could go there and see the plants and choose for themselves on the basis of personal inspection. Others said that they would buy only from reputable mail-order firms, and in most instances the names quoted were McGredy and Wheatcroft. Among the reasons for buying from local firms were that the conditions were likely to be the same as in local gardens, roses could be seen in bloom so that there could be no misunderstanding about colour, ordering could be done on impulse, a single plant could be bought as easily as many, plants

could be bought late in the season, there was no postage to pay, and so forth. On the other hand those who bought by mail-order believed that they got more perfect roses.

It was interesting to know that gardening appeared to be the main interest of more people in the north than in the south, and roses and other plants, and their effect, were a more frequent topic of conversation in the north. For these people it was important that plants should have a long flowering season, as modern roses do have, so that for months there would always be some colour in the garden. For most of the respondents the advantage of roses was that they were long-lived and the death of a plant was a comparatively rare thing. Importance was attached to the fact that there was no fear of ruining the plant while digging a bed, as there was with bulbs. All this was clear, that roses were beautiful, the perfect flower, and in many instances sweetly perfumed, and, what was important, roses were not demanding in the amount of care needed to maintain them and to make them grow.

The characteristic of the modern world in which mail-order has declined was apparent from these reports. The interests of the modern affluent society are not those of the recent past, and its pleasures are different. Now, with one and sometimes two cars in a house, and the pleasure of travel extended by a caravan and perhaps also a boat, the house-owner (and garden-owner) prefers to get away in his spare time. If he wants something, then he wants it at once—his wants and interests have to be supplied, like his coffee, on the instant principle. Roses are ideal for his garden, since they require so little attention. If he wants to buy roses then he will get into his car, with his wife and his family, and they will have a pleasant day out by going to a local garden-centre and walking about among the plants and the flowers and choosing roses on the spot.

Mail-order will go on, there is no doubt of that, but on the new terms I have outlined, of high quality at appropriate prices. Mail-order plants are invariably selected from catalogues backed up by press advertising and by photographs in monochrome or colour that appear in the editorial columns of the gardening press and the national press from time to time, and especially at the times of shows.

Though I have mounted some costly campaigns, I do not in general advertise on a large scale—nor do other nurseries. The main object of advertising by rose nurseries is to generate requests for catalogues, and in this the result is satisfactory.

We get some strange letters at times, and people send us a lot of information that is irrelevant but which, once they have got to know that we are a friendly firm, they feel impelled to give us —about their illnesses, their troubles, and their successes, about their maiden aunts and their mothers-in-law, and so on. Some amusing letters come from Africa, signing off with a graceful flourish that I think must be a translation from a native language more courtly, more picturesque than English in Britain has become: 'I am writing you very lovingly, I am your brother in Christ.' We send catalogues to all these requests, including the courtly gentlemen in Africa, who may be poor men educated in a mission or important officials in business or in government— one cannot tell.

My catalogues are always printed in full colour, showing the hues of the roses as accurately as good commercial printing will allow. The colour pictures are reproduced from large colour transparencies by Jim Lyttle, who is the nephew of Tom Weir, who used to be my father's hybridizer. Jim has become so skilful in this specialized field—and it is much more difficult than it may appear—that now I have only to give him the roses I want to have photographed and leave the rest to him. Other nurseries may use different processes to print their catalogues, but I find that four-colour photogravure is the most satisfactory process for the quantity I need and for the time in which it has to be produced.

The design of the catalogue has differed from year to year, varying from the rather loose and brassy effort of an advertising agency to a design more appropriate to our high quality image. I print 200,000 copies of each edition of the catalogue and the cost of colour-printing and of paper goes up each year, as also does the cost of envelopes and the work of addressing them. More striking is what is happening to postal charges. We sent the last catalogue out under 2p stamps. The postal charge, we are told, may be raised to 4p, which means another £4,000, and it may go up again, with another £2,000 for every new penny.

At the present time I have two different catalogues. One is for roses only and for mail-order, and the other includes roses with other garden shrubs and is for my garden-centre at Derriaghy. In the past catalogues have been designed in the nursery, or by an advertising agency, and lately by me. At one time it was believed that the briefest description of a rose was, in this frenetic world, the best, so that people could read through a catalogue in a brief moment of their time. I now think that that is wrong. I have come to understand how people like to read about their hobbies and interests, like to pore over descriptions and recommendations, and sometimes over very technical matters. I now give a longer, more useful account of each rose with details of the awards it has won, of course, and of its parentage, and I let some of my enthusiasm for the rose appear, instead of writing a coldly clinical paragraph. I think the ideal is to write a description of a rose as though I were corresponding personally with each customer, and I am sure that this brings about a more friendly approach.

There are outlets other than the private garden, outlets for large quantities of roses. The parks market is important in some countries, and especially so in Germany, where a rose-grower may breed a rose especially for use in public parks. The qualities needed for such roses are sturdiness and floriferousness of the plant, a long flowering period, and as little need for attention and maintenance as possible. I have already gone into the sponsoring of roses and its relation to production. Large numbers of plants with a sponsor's name may be supplied to the sponsor and he or his firm will use them in beds to decorate the office or factory grounds, and perhaps send batches to customers as goodwill gifts. Such a rose may also be on sale to the public in the ordinary way, as Mullard Jubilee is. Another sponsor may take the whole production of a rose named for them, as in the case of my new rose, Coventry Cathedral. Another mass market is the premium offer, in which a commercial firm offers roses in exchange for coupons cut from packets. Bird's offered a free, unnamed red rose, supplied by Hortico of Spalding, in exchange for coupons from Angel Delight, and Crosse & Blackwell offered a McGredy rose for ten labels from cans of soup. The advantage of this system to the rose-grower is that he has a guarantee for a large number of roses at an agreed figure. In my case it was for 50,000 roses. With such a guarantee a first-class rose can be produced at less than the normal market price.

We all have in us an inbuilt reluctance to take immediate action, to make decisions, and advertising has in some manner to overcome this. Premium offers achieve their results by emphasizing the temporary nature of the offer, that all coupons must be sent by a certain date. General advertising in many cases seeks the same sense of urgency, of novelty; if you look through any series of advertisements, for soap or ships or sealing-wax, the word you will find most frequently used will be 'new', with an exclamation mark. The rose business is one in which there is always something new. It is the breeders' very purpose to produce novelties and to bring them to the market, but there are always in addition those roses that were new last year or in the previous years, and these go on selling. A rose remains in my catalogue for an average of seven years. After that the variety is either losing its vigour or the demand for it has begun to fall. A good rose, such as Mullard Jubilee, will go on selling for ten years or more; some roses in the past have remained available for more than twenty years, a few much longer than that. Of the fifty roses illustrated each year in the catalogue (more are included but not illustrated), five or six will be novelties. It will be obvious from this that the principal purpose of press advertising for roses must be to generate requests for catalogues. Only a very exceptional rose or exceptional circumstances will warrant an extensive individual campaign in the press. The two most remarkable examples were those for Peace and for Spartan. Peace, of course,

City of Belfast

was a rose in a million, and the American propagator Conard-Pyle was sufficiently wide-awake to realize this. He publicized it very efficiently and established Peace as the most famous rose of our time. Every newspaper and magazine carried the story of its origin in Meilland's nursery during the war and of the manner in which budding material was carried out of France to the United States in the diplomatic bag. At the San Francisco peace conference every delegate found a bowl of the new roses in his bedroom. It was a stroke of genius, at that time, to call the rose Peace—Meilland, as I have said, had wanted it to be called Mme Antoine Meilland. The result of the publicity, for a rose that deserved it (it is important in rose-breeding, as in other things, that the goods should stand up to the publicity image), is that Peace has sold more plants than any rose in history, and it is still selling strongly after thirty years. It is reputed to have brought Meilland a fortune in royalties.

The advertising campaign for Spartan was a different matter. Spartan was—and is—an excellent rose and Charlie Perkins confidently expected it to win the All America trials. In fact it did not win, but Charlie Perkins was not going to let that dismay him. In his opinion his rose was the best and he was going to make sure that everyone else thought so too. He spent hundreds of thousands of dollars in one week-end on full-colour pages in *Life*, in *Time*, in the *Saturday Evening Post*, and I don't know where else. He could never have got his money back in sales, but he persuaded everybody that Spartan was *the* rose of that year, he made all America talk about it and recognize it, and that was what he wanted. He was content.

Direct advertising in the press is not the only way of publicizing a rose or a rose-grower. There is also the medley of operations that go under the title of public relations. Every rose-grower had practised this kind of publicity for years without knowing that it had a name, and indeed before it had a name. We have all of us been in the habit of persuading the press to print in the editorial columns descriptions of new roses or of newsworthy events, and from time to time we have all of us managed to have pictures of roses in full colour outside on covers or inside in the text. We have all given occasional parties to celebrate something or other, or to attract attention. All this was public relations, though we did not know it. It was not until after the last war that the name came into general use and that the business was organized as an advisory and publicity-getting service.

I encountered professional P.R. for the first time in the person of Bob Aylwin, to whom I was introduced in Fleet Street in the late fifties. I found him a very interesting man. He had been P.R.O. for Bertram Mills's circus for ten years, until he was knocked out by a severe illness. When I met him he was just beginning to get back into his stride after that disaster. I was young at that time and very green and I was easily persuaded that I ought to have a P.R. man. I realize now that I was lucky in meeting a man like Bob who knew his job, rather than some pseudo fellow who would take my money without doing very much for it. Bob said he would give me a demonstration of how P.R. worked, and he called up two or three of his friends among the journalists of Fleet Street. They came round straight away to interview me and we had a convivial half-hour's talk. Sure enough, in the morning there were paragraphs about Sam McGredy and his roses in the newspapers. I was impressed. Perhaps the demonstration was always laid on ready to dazzle potential clients, but I signed Bob up straight away, at first for a year, and then for another year, and in the event Bob remained as P.R. man for McGredy's nursery for a period of ten years.

He had a lot of sound ideas and he did some very good things for me. He was responsible for the arrangements that led up to the naming of the Evelyn Fison rose for Fisons and we did a lot of business from that—I sold a quarter of a million roses in one year. He was responsible also for obtaining permission from the Queen Mother for me to name a rose Elizabeth of Glamis. It was he too who persuaded Violet Carson ('Ena Sharples') to allow us to use her name for a rose. In fact, Bob Aylwin did a lot of things for me, and what I have learned about P.R. came from him. Nowadays I do much of the public relations for the nursery myself.

Bob used occasionally to come with me to rose functions and one of these was to the Festival of Kerry, which is held annually at Tralee. During the festival a girl is elected to be the Rose of Tralee for the year—the title, of course, comes from the familiar song, which was written by a man called William Mulchinock, who died in 1864. My involvement was to name a rose the Rose of Tralee—there had never been a Rose of Tralee in the flower sense before. Maureen and I and Bob went down to the first of the festivals. The festival began with a big parade from Shannon airport through about eighty miles of countryside, stopping at nearly every bar on the way, or so it seems in retrospect. Bob had been handling roses before we started out and he had got a sizeable thorn in his finger. On the way to Tralee the finger began to throb badly and to swell, and as the day wore on it got worse and he was in considerable pain. So someone was sent on ahead to the next town to ask for a doctor to be ready to treat him. When he got there the doctor took Bob up to a room in a pub, examined the finger, filled a syringe from a phial, commanded Bob to take down his trousers, and rammed the needle into his backside. For some reason Bob picked up the empty phial and put it into his pocket. 'What do I owe you?' he said as he buttoned up his trousers. The doctor said Bob could just come downstairs and buy him a drink; that was all that would be necessary. So they sought the bar and Bob, already beginning to feel better, bought the doctor his drink. As he rejoined the parade and we left the town the pain had disappeared completely, and wondering what magic substance had been injected into him Bob took the phial out of his pocket and looked at the label. It said: 'Commercial sample—not to be used after 1952.'

That visit was my introduction to the county of Kerry and to the wonderful people who live in that south-west corner of Ireland. We have been back every year, Maureen and I, and now we two personally as well as McGredy's nursery must be well known down there. It led, too, to my calling a rose Kerryman, as I have explained in the previous chapter.

The Americans were the real masters of public relations,

especially in my earlier days, and among them Jackson & Perkins stood out. They were the first people to have a rose-garden and to throw it open to the public, and the first people to found an international flower-arrangement competition. Charlie Perkins lived in a big old house in Newark, and there he entertained lavishly, with a bar manned by a black barman whose name was Sandstorm. Every year they would have two weeks of jollifications for the benefit of the press, with the bar set out on the lawn behind the house. Hundreds of people, thousands maybe, would tramp straight through the house to circulate on the lawn and get their drinks from Sandstorm. There were pressmen there of all kinds, experts come to judge the flower competition, and people like me who had been persuaded to get up on their feet and say a few kind words about J. & P. roses.

I suppose that you could say that the printing of pictures of me in my catalogues and in various places in the general press is all included in public relations operations—it forms part of the image that the public have of the firm. If, when they see a rose, they have a picture of a field of roses with Sam McGredy standing in the middle of it, then they think of Sam McGredy's roses, and that cannot but be beneficial to me. I hope I look amiable and trustworthy in those pictures, and if I do, then that is all to the good, for a firm like mine lives, and will continue to live, on the trust of its customers. This kind of publicity has some odd consequences, however. People regard me as a rose expert able to diagnose and suggest a cure for all the ills of their roses, just as a doctor finds himself constantly being tapped for free advice. My customers recognize me from my pictures, and buttonhole me with such questions as: 'Can you tell me what is wrong with my Mrs. Sam McGredy climber?—it isn't climbing the way it should.' Questions about pruning constantly recur; despite the instructions in many books and magazines, pruning remains a subject that resists general understanding.

I do not have a good memory for faces—in any case, in my kind of business I see so many faces that I could not possibly remember them all—and I am frequently baffled by some person

I do not recognize hailing me as though I should know him. For instance, at a Rotary Club meeting the other day three or four people came up and shook hands with me without my having any idea who they were. They could have been customers, or they could have been people I had met some years before. When I think I recognize someone as an acquaintance I am unsure whether he really is an acquaintance or someone whose face I have seen on television or at a show. Recently I was having lunch with Seán Jennett in a West End restaurant in London when a man at the next table leaned across, saying to his partner: 'I must shake hands with Sam.' I still have no idea who he was. Incidents of this sort make me feel guilty. The most bizarre of such occasions, with no feeling of guilt on my part, occurred when Maureen and I were on holiday in Majorca. We were lying on the beach browning in the Mediterranean sun. With my panama over my face to keep the glare off I was gently dozing away when I heard a family nearby discussing me quite clearly. 'I'm sure that's Sam McGredy,' said the man. 'No, it isn't,' said his wife. 'I'll bet it is,' the man replied, and his wife said, 'Well, go over and see.' With that the chap just got up, came over, lifted the hat from my face, and asked: 'Are you Sam McGredy?' 'Yes,' I said, 'how do you do?'

I arrange cocktail and other parties from time to time to launch an important new rose or publicize some event or other. Bob Aylwin stage-managed many of these parties and got important or influential people to come along. I remember too a priceless coup he pulled off when we launched the rose for my sister Paddy McGredy. TV viewers saw the newscaster of that time, Tim Brinton, reading the news with a splendid rose in his button-hole. At the end of the news Tim said: 'You may wonder why I have this rose in my buttonhole. Well, it is a new variety from the Chelsea Flower Show, called Paddy McGredy. And here is Paddy McGredy herself,' and the camera panned over to show my sister seated behind a great bowl of Paddy McGredy roses. The publicity was immense, and after that we had thousands of people coming to the show and asking to see the new Paddy

McGredy rose. We had our launching party afterwards, with Paddy there, and of course there was lots of Paddy whiskey, and many other Irish things, and every guest was given a shillelagh to remind him of the occasion.

Another party of a special kind was one I gave at the Waldorf Hotel in London. Everything was to do with roses. There were rose-petal sandwiches, rose ice-cream, Turkish coffee with rose-water, and a rose cocktail. The last of these was a potent Bulgarian liqueur made from rose petals and spirits, kindly provided from his personal stock by the Bulgarian minister to London. There were also herring-roes on toast, which my guests ate, I hope, without realizing what a terrible pun it was. Each of the women among the guests was sent off at the end of the party with a box of chocolates filled with rose-flavoured cream, and topped with real crystallized rose petals from McGredy roses. I remember that Orangeade was one of the new roses introduced on that occasion.

There is no real division in rose-growing between what is essentially marketing and what is not. From the very beginning the sheer aesthetic pleasure of creating something new in the long process of breeding must be enjoyed in the context of what is saleable. If it were otherwise, if the pleasure and the triumph came first in importance, rose-breeding would be a costly hobby, not a profession and a business. The sending of roses to trials and to shows, the winning of awards—everything is aimed in a single direction. Even my Better Roses Club is basically sales orientated, though it gives a great many expert gardeners—about three thousand of them—the pleasure and privilege of growing new McGredy roses not yet on the market and of observing and judging them. I founded the McGredy Better Roses Club in the mid-sixties. The members receive rose plants from me, numbered but unnamed, a year before they go on the market, and they judge the qualities of each plant and evaluate their decisions by so many points out of a hundred. I average out the pointing and I find that a rose that averages eighty points has to be a very good rose indeed, while one that gets ninety points must be superlative.

What this club does is not only to give me these point-ratings for my roses, it also helps me to get the feel of the market for any particular rose and this is taken into account in my planning and propagating programmes.

The regular trials, such as those of the Royal National Rose Society and the many foreign ones, serve the same purpose with the additional advantage of showing how my roses are regarded by experts in competition with those of other breeders.

There are strictly two categories of rose-shows or rose-festivals. The Chelsea Flower Show is the exemplar of one kind, where keen gardeners come to see what is new, to discuss matters with their favourite supplier, and, if they wish, to place an order at once for any variety they admire. The other kind is represented by many Continental shows, which are really spectacles, or expositions, with great masses of one variety of plants or of one colour. A display in one of these expositions is very expensive to mount and to maintain, since some of these shows, like that at the I.G.A. in Hamburg, go on for months. The visitors are people come for a day out, to see and to enjoy the beauty and the colour. They do not come to buy, because you cannot buy anything from these events; there is no organization directed at sales. All you can do is to note the names of nurserymen and perhaps ask them to send catalogues. These shows are in reality public-relations exercises. The show at Valenciennes, in the mining and steel-manufacturing district of the Département du Nord, north of Paris, the I.G.A. in Hamburg, and the Floriade in Holland are of similar kind. They are held every so many years, ranging from every two years for Vincennes in Paris to every ten years for the Floriade in Rotterdam. Such shows are much more extensive than Chelsea, with great beds of roses and other flowers. In the past I have chartered aeroplanes to take sufficient roses to the Continental shows.

The show at Valenciennes has personal and happy memories for me because it was the first foreign show I attended after I had taken over the direction of the nursery from my Uncle Walter. I went on from there to Paris for another meeting, which was delayed, and I had a week in Paris all by myself and with nothing to do but what pleased me. I was very young and I really fell for the charm of Paris, so that all I needed to do to have a marvellous and memorable time was to idle about the streets and the squares in the clear spring sunshine, observing and being part of the Parisian bustle and movement. Or I would buy a lump of cheese and piece of bread in the morning and go off for the whole 'ay along the embankments of the *rive gauche* or the *rive droite*, stupidly happy to walk there beside the water and under the trees and to talk to other strollers and to anglers and to whoever could understand me. It was enjoyable to wander in the sunshine or lean on the parapets of embankments or bridges to examine the opaque Seine with all the concentration it deserves.

I am sad to have to say that flower-shows in Great Britain are dying out. We used to exhibit at twenty-five flower-shows in these islands, but last year the number was down to five, and in future I shall probably exhibit at only one—the Chelsea Flower Show of course—with perhaps some seedlings at the Royal National Rose Show. It is not that attendances are going down— they are, but not seriously; more marked is the decline in the value of orders placed at these shows, which has been such that shows will in future have to be regarded as public-relations ventures as far as the rose-grower is concerned. Public relations have taken a hard knock in these last few years. I shall go on with some Continental shows; McGredy's will be represented at Rotterdam in 1972 and the following year at Hamburg, which is very important.

Rose trial-grounds such as Belfast's in Ireland and Bagatelle in Paris are also shows to which the public may be admitted, but they are different from flower festivals. They are better called rose *concours*, where roses compete and may be compared, both by the official judges for the pointing and by the public for their own interest. As I have already said, there are trial-grounds throughout the world—in Paris, Madrid, The Hague, Baden-Baden, Copenhagen, Rome, Geneva, and in the United States, as well as the grounds of the Royal National Rose Society in England. Each

Satchins

trial-ground takes six plants from each breeder, for each variety to be tested, and over the following two years the plants are examined periodically by a competent jury or panel of judges and are awarded points according to their quality.

There is no doubt that every city throughout the world would love to have its own trial-ground, for with all the roses sent each year, which are kept and planted out in parks, they would soon build up magnificent and up-to-date rose-gardens at no capital cost for the plants. Rose-breeders, however, are not inclined to allow trial-grounds to multiply without clear evidence of benefit to their business. One of the more recent of trial-grounds is that in Belfast, in Dixon Park, and this is the one to which my heart is given because I was instrumental in founding it. I believe that it is today the best in Europe and I doubt whether the United States can show anything superior.

It came about in this way. Some years ago I tried to persuade Lord Brookborough, who was then Prime Minister of Northern Ireland, that a trial-ground in Belfast would be a success, and he was interested. Unfortunately I could not at that time get sufficient support from other rose-breeders and the project failed to mature. A year or two later I talked on this subject with Craig Wallace, who had been at Reading University at the same time as myself and who had joined the Department of Horticulture in the Ministry of Agriculture. He had conceived the notion of founding a Northern Ireland rose society and was looking for some suitable peg on which to hang it. It seemed a wild idea. There was the Royal National Rose Society with a hundred thousand members out of a population of fifty million, and here were we, Craig Wallace and I, discussing the possibility of a viable society in a population of less than two millions. I had to tell Craig that I could not help him in this venture because if I had a hand in it there would be too many people who would say that I did it solely for the sake of the publicity the McGredy nursery would get out of it. I suggested that instead it would be better to organize an international trial-ground. He accepted that idea and went off to work on it, and in no time he had inspired enthusiasm in the Department of Agriculture and in Reg Wesley, Belfast Parks Superintendent, who would have charge of the trial-ground. The city fathers said they would supply and maintain the ground. So there we were, the two of us, with the decision made and the initiative passed back to us to make it a reality. We did just that, or rather Craig Wallace did, for it was he who managed all the large amount of work and organization necessary. Today Belfast has a wonderful trial-ground and a rose-garden with better spectacle than its rivals have because the conditions on which roses are accepted for trial were deliberately made different. First, it was required that breeders should submit twenty-five plants of each variety, instead of the six that are required elsewhere; and second, plants for trial should be submitted in the year in which they go on sale, instead of two years before. The importance of this latter rule is that in the year of launching the breeder has built up a stock and can more easily afford the twenty-five plants required. The plants are judged and pointed as usual, but with the addition of a final pointing by an international committee, who provide ten per cent of the points.

The result is that the City of Belfast's rose-garden is now one of the finest sights of the city, with more than twenty thousand roses in it. They bloom in a magnificent setting, on undulating ground with the Antrim mountains sweeping up behind for a backcloth.

The City of Belfast is very proud of its rose-garden, as well it may be, and every year the corporation puts up a lavish luncheon for rose notabilities, and often the government entertains us at Stormont in the Parliament House. The Rose Society is supported also by other authorities, including the Milk Marketing Board, and by private firms, notably Richardson's, the big fertilizer company. Now we have a Northern Ireland Rose Society with about three hundred members and we have a bigger and I think better trial-ground than the Royal National Rose Society has at St. Albans. The whole organization is provided by the Rose Society of Northen Ireland.

The success of the rose trial-ground in Belfast naturally aroused a desire in Dublin for one of their own. They asked me if I could help, but I had to say to them that Ireland is a small country, and while we had been fortunate to persuade rose-breeders to support Belfast, it was highly unlikely that they would support another trial-ground in Ireland. Since then Birmingham and Newcastle, in England, have tried to found trial-grounds, but they have had no success, despite the much larger populations they would serve.

All the same, rose trial-grounds have increased in number, though in general only one in each country succeeds. There are now trial-grounds in Paris, Geneva, Madrid, Rome, Baden-Baden, Hamburg, Courtrai, The Hague, Copenhagen, Palmerston North, New Zealand, and Tokyo. The United States is dominated by the All-America Rose Selection organization, which has twenty-two trial-grounds scattered across the country in all kinds of climates. My only criticism of this is that there are too many trial-grounds grouped in southern California, but that is because there is a large number of nurseries there. The number of plants required is the same as is general in Europe, and they are grown in a similar manner, but they are scored by regional committees all over the States. The scorings are gathered together by the All-America Selection Committee and are averaged. This is where the system becomes awkward for the breeder. The rose with the highest points usually wins, but not necessarily so—the organization is a commercial undertaking, and it will lean towards a rose that it believes will be a success on the market. Again, it may be seen at the end of the first year of trials that a rose is building up such a lead in points that it seems likely to win or at least to be in the first four for hybrid teas, for floribundas, or for grandifloras, etc., and then the breeder has to take the decision to build up a stock of that plant to meet the possible demand. This means budding perhaps five thousand plants and growing them to a stage when they will be ready for the market. At the end of the second year it may seem certain that the rose is going to win and the breeder has to risk increasing his stock to fifty thousand plants. Then the final judging is done and he finds that his rose has been beaten by some such imperceptible margin as ·02 of a point, and that is enough to make a great deal of difference in sales.

The only other trial I know of in the U.S.A. is the one in Portland, Oregon. Oregon has a fine mild climate, rather like that of Northern Ireland, but drier, and roses do well there. Portland runs a big municipal garden on a rose-trials basis. Other cities that have good rose-gardens are Tyler in Texas, Washington, San Francisco, and others—in fact most big American cities have a municipal rose-garden, but not all are run on a trials basis.

I have the right to send to Portland any varieties I want. I suppose that as much as 40 per cent of the roses there are mine, and that makes me feel very affectionate about Portland, Oregon. I go over there most years just to have a look at the garden.

Another very interesting garden is that of Palmerston North in New Zealand, the country in which the first meeting of the World Rose Convention is to be held in the fall of 1971, in the city of Hamilton. The convention was founded at a meeting in London about four years ago, with delegates coming from many countries, including Australia and New Zealand. An international convention committee was set up, and it was this committee that decided to hold the first world convention in New Zealand, the first of a series that would be held at three-year intervals, with each meeting in a different country. The second convention is to be held in Chicago in 1974, the third in London in 1977.

New Zealand was a good choice for the first convention, showing a fine impartiality and demonstrating that the big countries and the big cities were not going to be allowed to dominate the selection of meeting-places. It was a good choice, too, because New Zealand has a perfect climate for roses and the plants grow there to the very best condition—you never saw such roses as they grow in New Zealand. As the centre of the first World Rose Convention, New Zealand decided that it must put itself firmly on the rose map and the natural decision was to found a rose trial-ground. A fact-finding delegation was sent to Europe, and we were flattered, in Northern Ireland, because they came to Belfast and decided that the trial-ground there was

Mullard Jubilee

the best and their new ground should be based on it. The Northern Ireland Rose Society gave them considerable help. They had fixed on Palmerston North, north of Wellington in North Island, because that is a particularly good growing area, and this was convenient for me because my agent lives only about thirty miles away. It was decided that the first trial should take place a year before the convention, that is in 1970, and it made me very happy that the gold medal for the hybrid tea went to Pania, which is one of my roses, and the gold medal for the floribunda was won by City of Belfast, which is another of my roses.

Stripping the poll—that is, winning all the major awards in any competition—is very difficult and is superlative publicity. I have done it three times. In New Zealand there were only two gold medals. At The Hague, in 1970, the award for the best hybrid tea went to Mullard Jubilee, for the best floribunda to Satchmo, for the best fragrant rose to Lady Seton, and for the best rose in the whole garden during the last five years to Jan Spek. That triumph brought a lump to my throat that day because all the trade was there, all my competitors, and they had all submitted new roses for trial. But best of all, my old friend Jan Spek—the first friend I made on the Continent, after whom I had named the rose—he was there to see his namesake acclaimed as the very best rose among so many. Curiously, the rose had not done very well in Britain—in fact it had been adversely criticized by many people, but it had won the Belfast trials. It is a beautiful rose that seems to like the Irish climate. And it had won in Holland for Jan Spek, and that was marvellous. I have a picture of Jan going forward with me to receive the medal, both of us very proud.

The only other time I have stripped the poll was in 1963 in Great Britain, when Elizabeth of Glamis won the President's Trophy as the best rose of the year, together with the Clay Cup for the best fragrant rose, Casino got the gold medal for a climber (the first climber in years to get a gold medal), and Evelyn Fison got the gold medal for a red floribunda. There was great excitement. Nobody had ever done all that before.

Of course, I am moved and exhilarated by such triumphs, and

I like to receive a cup or a gold medal as well as anyone, but I could not possibly keep all that I win. I have some of the medals in a bag in the loft. The cups I re-dedicate. I have the lettering taken off them and new lettering engraved and they become Sam McGredy cups to be won by members of amateur rose societies—another example of useful P.R. activity. As for gold medals, McGredy's nursery had won a lot of them before I came along—the mayoral chain of Portadown, presented by my mother, is composed of gold medals won by McGredy roses.

The President's Trophy came my way four times, once with Mischief, once with Elizabeth of Glamis, then with City of Belfast, and again with Molly McGredy. The purse that went with such an important trophy was very small—only twenty-five pounds. You did not get the money; instead the winner was asked to choose something to be presented to him. The honour is worth thousands of pounds in sales and royalties, but all you got as a prize was the value of twenty-five pounds. When I won it with Elizabeth of Glamis I was away, but Maureen was told by telephone that she should choose something to be presented. She went out and bought a cut-glass rose-bowl. That was fine, and it looked good passing from the hands of the president into mine on the rostrum. Then I got the award again with City of Belfast and I was asked once more to choose something to be presented to me. A day or so later I was in Liberty's in Regent Street in London, when I saw two big and heavy ashtrays in smoky orange glass, and I thought how much I would like them. I communed with myself and decided 'Why not?', so I bought them on the spot, adding five pounds to make up the price of thirty pounds. On the day of the presentation I marched up to the platform to be presented with my two glass ashtrays, and I have a strong impression that I had offended against the code and had not done quite the right thing. Then I won the award again, with Molly McGredy. This time I used the twenty-five pounds to buy Maureen a rose-quartz ring, and that was presented to me as before. The truth of the matter is that with an honour such as the President's Trophy no cash prize is really necessary or could be adequate, and that has been recognized. Now there is the permanent trophy, which the winner keeps for a year, and with it you get a replica to keep for yourself. Nobody really wants the twenty-five pounds, and perhaps no one really wants the replica; what I at least like is simply the honour of having bred the best rose in Britain for that year, and I would like the name of the breeder and the name of the winning rose to be printed in the National Rose Society's annual, in a list, just as they print the names of past presidents.

Different trials have different prizes. The Golden Rose of The Hague is a huge medal with a large golden rose in relief in the centre. The City of Belfast has three prizes—a golden brooch, a gold medal, and a great golden thorn about eight inches high. All these things are very grand, but when you have won one you don't always want to have another. The golden brooch is the award for fragrance, and now when rose-breeding families meet at some rose occasion, each wife sports the golden brooch— Maureen has one, Kordes' wife has one, Edward le Grice's wife another. My rose City of Belfast won the City of Belfast trial in 1970, an achievement of which I was especially proud. When the mayor presented me with the Golden Thorn, the second I had won, I turned round and gave it to Craig Wallace in recognition of his work in founding the City of Belfast trials. He was speechless!

Whatever one's private joy in winning such awards as these may be, for the breeder the real monetary value is in the effect a first-class award has on the sales of the rose concerned. People naturally expect roses that have won such awards to have high qualities of form or fragrance, and that is why all rose-breeders and rose-propagators emphasize the awards in their sales catalogues. The awards are powerful supports of advertising and publicity.

Colourful and beautiful as roses may be, intriguing and romantic and creative as the breeding of new roses certainly is, every rose-breeder and rose-grower works for one mundane purpose, and that is to make a *profit*. There can be, or could be, a great deal of money to be made in roses, as the massive operations of Jackson & Perkins showed, and there is still money to be made, despite the recession in this business in the later 1960s. I have already dealt with the system of sponsoring roses. The £10,000 for Mullard Jubilee is the largest sum ever paid in cash for sponsoring a rose in any country. From that superb rose and high level of finance, we descend through a diminishing scale down to the annual cases of whisky from Arthur Bell.

The quickest way to make money, if you have the kind of luck that wins in lotteries, is in the breeding of greenhouse roses for commercial growing. This serves the market for cut-blooms, and it can be worth a lot of money. You could be a millionaire in no time if everything went right for you in this specialized branch of the rose business, but the risks, too, are great and I do not care to venture into it. The star of greenhouse roses is Baccara, which was bred by Meilland. The qualities needed for a greenhouse rose are long stems, which allow for a tall vase, and the ability to live for a long time in water after cutting. It has to produce a lot of blooms per square metre and most important of all, the public have to like it and *demand* it. Greenhouse-growers buy plants by the thousand and even tens of thousands and that is why there is a lot of money in breeding greenhouse roses. There are dangers too. The trade either wants a rose or it does not want it at all—there are no half-measures here—so the breeder may have instant success or instant failure. The failures can be very expensive, years of breeding and all it has cost gone in a moment or two—and that a great deal. What a breeder wagers is those six or seven years of breeding plus the value of the stock he has had to build up to be ready for the demand he hoped for. A man is lucky if he breeds one successful greenhouse rose in a lifetime. This trade is very different from the garden-rose business that is my speciality.

The market for garden roses has not yet fully settled down after the upsets of the sixties, but it appears that equilibrium is in sight. The mail-order business will go on and it will, at least as far as I am concerned, be a market for super-quality plants.

The one thing I am sure will go on with less change than in the rest of the rose business is the breeding of roses, and this is the field that I think of as notably the one in which I live and work, though in fact any rose-breeder, if he is going to survive, must be something of a salesman as well.

The operation for the launching of a new rose is simply a combination of the various methods of publicity I have already mentioned, taken to a higher level of concentration in a shorter time. Advertising, publicity through public relations, press hand-outs, and photographs, the culmination of the pointing systems of my Better Roses Club and of the various trial-grounds, and emphasis on any awards the rose may have won, all these efforts are concentrated upon the new rose. There are cocktail parties such as I have described, attended by the press and a sprinkling of V.I.P.s. Notably, I mount a pre-Chelsea cocktail party. Then I have a McGredy flower-arrangement competition throughout the country, with heats in all the flower-shows. The finalist wins a splendid cup and we bring him or her to the Savoy Hotel in London to arrange our roses there. That is only one of my publicity ploys. The press is encouraged in every possible way to take notice of the new rose. In general, the more bally-hoo and brouhaha we can make about a new rose the better, and in the end its image and its news-value are firmly implanted in the minds of all those who matter.

Then there are heaven-sent incidents that are beloved by the press. For instance, if the rose Elizabeth of Glamis is seen by the Queen Mother and she sniffs it and is photographed, then that picture and the name of the rose will be in every paper. Then again, if Ginger Rogers happens to be playing in London in a successful play about the time of the launch of a rose named after her, a similar situation arises, in which the rose is linked with the star and benefits by her fame.

Sometimes it is necessary to point out very carefully to the press in what manner a rose is new and what is newsworthy about it. If it is something startling and obvious, as a blue rose would be, then you would have nothing to do to get notice other than to display it at some major show, such as Chelsea, and publicity will expand from it like ripples from a stone in water. To use another metaphor, the tide will be running for you and it will be difficult for anyone else to compete with another rose. This is important, for I should point out that there is a limited market for new roses. Every year several breeders bring out new roses and what each of them wants to do is to capture his share of the market and as much more as possible. If a customer has, say, only about five pounds to spend on new roses, and if he has thirty or forty roses from different breeders to choose from, then I want him to buy my roses and not Dickson's or Tantau's or those of someone else. That is not selfish. It is good business to capture as much of the market as one can and any firm that does not set out to do this is not a healthy firm, or won't be for long.

7. PLUNDER AND PROTECTION

The rose business, I am glad to say, is comparatively free from fraud and other evil practices that beset so many commercial and financial enterprises, but most rose-breeders and rose-growers have at some time had experience of the seamier side of the trade.

Bad faith in observing contracts is one thing that has occurred, and an important example of this came about as follows. In the early 1930s my father went to the States to work out a contract for the sale of his roses through the agency of an American nursery. No agreement or contract can be completely water-tight; it must depend to some extent on good will for its proper implementation, and in fact my father's contract worked well for a long time, and other European breeders signed contracts with the Americans along similar lines. For years American catalogues contained pages of McGredy roses and showed also roses from other breeders. But after the war a few Americans began to 'bury' European roses for which they had the rights under these contracts. By that I mean that they ceased to advertise them and to show them, so that there were no sales and consequently no royalties for European breeders. That was at a time when the U.S.A. was supreme in the rose world. They had so much money that they could buy anything they wanted. Occasionally their plant-hunters would make a progress through Europe like visiting potentates, buying whatever took their eye in the way of new varieties; but they did not always do anything with them when they got back to the States. If a rose bought like this was not marketed it meant that the European grower had lost the American market for that particular rose and it was never seen again on that side of the Atlantic. A notable example of this process was

Iceberg, a Kordes rose which has been acknowledged to be the best white rose in existence, so the loss was America's as well as Europe's.

Those of us whose roses were 'buried' could do nothing but be jealous, for the contracts contained clauses giving American agents the right, if the contracts were broken, to exploit exclusively for a period of seven years all the seedlings in their possession.

All this is past history and the arguments and the bitterness are ended now. At that time the Americans had the lead and the impetus in rose-breeding and in selling roses, and that was because they were the first to have and to benefit by a system of plant patents. Today the scene is different. Europe has plant patents and royalty rights now, and I would say that pre-eminence in the rose industry now belongs on the European side of the ocean. European breeders as a whole have proved somewhat more perceptive in the breeding of new roses.

Before the arrival of plant patents and royalty rights the picture presented by the rose industry was very curious and essentially about a hundred years behind the times. It was possible, in effect, for anybody to copy a rose, that is to propagate it, with impunity and with no legal need to pay a penny to anybody. In any definition, moral or commercial, this was piracy, but it was piracy within the law, and in fact it was the entire basis on which the propagating nurseries were founded and became prosperous. If royalties were ever paid, as in a few instances they were, it was by 'gentleman's agreement' and not by legal compulsion.

The absence of breeders' rights encouraged offences ranging from ordinary theft to blatant exploitation. The former was a crime and punishable by law if the miscreant was found; the latter was legal without redress.

Simple theft might be encountered wherever roses were exhibited or were accessible to the public. Once, at a show in Shrewsbury, I lost a whole bush of Piccadilly, and the lack of that bush meant that I could not win the premier award, as I and other knowledgeable people were confident I should have done. The thief may have been some penurious amateur or rose-enthusiast, but he could have been a rival grower stealing to obtain budding material so that he could propagate plants to be sold on the open market. No evidence that I know of turned up to show that he was of the latter class. Another time, when I was showing at Balmoral, no less than two hundred of my roses disappeared. A theft on that scale baffles me. All those roses, one might suppose, could have been of use only to someone in the trade, but in those days anyone who wanted to propagate a variety in commercial quantities needed only to buy one or two plants in the ordinary way. By the time a new variety had got as far as exhibition in a show the wraps were off and any protection or guard was off as well. By that time the rose was available to anyone who could pay for it. It could, of course, be said that these thefts were intended to nobble my exhibits and so to prevent me from winning the awards for which I was competing. If that was the case, I could at least have consoled myself with the knowledge that it is generally the favourite that is nobbled.

It would be more reasonable to suggest nefarious intent by a propagator if the roses had been stolen from my nursery or from a trial-ground at a time before they were launched on to the general market. I have no doubt that such thefts have occurred. The motive would be the advantage to be gained by marketing a new variety at the same time or even ahead of the breeder. Any simpleton might steal from a nursery, but if what he was after was an important new variety he would have to know exactly where it was and what it looked like. This information he might extract without much difficulty. He would only have to present himself at a nursery and ask nicely to be shown around and, rose-breeders in general being courteous people and proud of what they do, he would be shown around all right. With a few innocent questions he would get to know what he wanted and in the morning at first light the fellow would creep back and cut off a stem or two with buds on them. In those stems he would have all that would be needed to start propagating that variety of rose.

That instance suggests that rose-breeders do not protect their roses in the field. Of course, we do, and any thief would need a bit more than ordinary luck to get clean away with it. We cannot do anything to protect those of our roses growing in trial-grounds. There we have to leave the matter to the authorities concerned. Bud material has in the past been abstracted from trial-grounds. I recall an instance concerning a rose called Rumba, which was bred by Niels Poulsen and for which I was his agent in Britain. So Niels had budding stock and I had budding stock, and we were busy propagating sufficient quantities for the launch, but before either of us could put Rumba on the market it appeared from a third source. Someone had acquired bud material from a trial-ground in the U.S.A. and had brought it to Britain via Bermuda. To avoid a thing like that you would have to catch the delinquent in the act. Otherwise it would be very difficult to prove anything, and in this particular instance it would have involved expensive legal entanglements across two continents.

Before the advent of plant patents and plant breeders' rights there was no offence, nothing illegal or unusual in propagating any new variety provided that the grower had obtained his bud material legitimately, and that he could do by simple purchase of a plant or bush at any time after the variety had been launched. All the propagating nurseries lived in this way, by buying a plant or two and taking buds from them and grafting them on to root-stocks, and so multiplying the numbers. The quantities they could raise were startling. In general, the original breeder had a head start on the market, but that start was not more than a few months, or at best one to two years. The more successful his new rose promised to be the quicker were the nurserymen to begin budding. A classic example of what could be done concerned the rose Queen Elizabeth. It is a good rose and with that name it was bound to be a success. It was propagated to the number of thirty or forty thousand plants in the space of three winter months. This feat was achieved by growing the plants in hot, damp peat in a super-heated greenhouse. In this way grafted stock can be made to set and to grow more buds in as little as three weeks, and every following five weeks the process is repeated, and there is a tremendous multiplication. There was nothing illegal in that, nothing out of the ordinary except the speed of the operation, and the propagator had no obligation, legal or moral, to pay a penny to the breeder of that rose.

The matter is different now. The U.S.A. has had a patent law for plants, based on the common industrial patent, since 1930. It stopped the former legal piracy of roses in the States and as a consequence the U.S. rose industry became very important and prosperous. The picture in Europe was less orderly. There was no similar protection in European countries, and from about 1950 onwards there was agitation in several of those countries for a plants patents bill and for plant-breeders' rights. As I have said, Francis Meilland was a moving spirit in bringing the need for protection of the plant-breeding industry to the notice of European governments, and in Britain Dickson, Le Grice, and I were constantly hammering at authority. Meilland travelled all over Europe to argue and to plead his case, and if the success of the movement may be attributed to any one man then it is to be attributed to him. Sadly, he did not live long enough to enjoy it, for, as I have said, he died of cancer while still a young man.

In Britain, we did at last, in 1964, obtain plant variety rights legislation, and the Plant Variety Rights Office was set up. From that time breeders have enjoyed protection for their plants and for the names by which they have called them. It entitled breeders to license others to propagate their new roses. That legislation made it more difficult for pirates to propagate in advance and to market in competition with the breeder, and they could not use the name without agreement. Protection, however, has proved to be expensive: it costs £60 in the first year of the variety and £30 per year afterwards through a period of fifteen years (if the variety lasts as long as that). That means nearly £500 for a single variety. If the rose proved a good seller, the fees might look comparatively small, but if it did not, the cost of the patent could loom large in its account. With new roses coming every year a breeder quickly accumulated a string of patents and the outgoings multiplied. In Europe, money could be saved by simply registering the name as a trade-mark, without taking out a patent, at a cost of a few pounds; the trade-mark gives some protection, if not as much as would a patent.

Plant variety rights specifications for roses are, as it were, illustrated in the garden of the Royal National Rose Society at St. Albans, where a growing collection of protected roses is maintained. The conditions for the grant of rights are simple, and number three only: the rose must be distinct from any other; it must be uniform, which is to say that one plant and flower must be like another; and it must be stable, with no tendency to revert to something else. Quality is not regarded; a rose may have all kinds of faults and defects, and it may be subject to mildew and any other disease—if it satisfies the three basic requirements it can be protected.

The most important thing for the breeder, the most important in my lifetime, was this international recognition of plant-breeders' rights. An international convention in Paris in 1961 resulted in the definition of these rights and their recognition at first in four countries and later in many others. Britain was first to ratify the convention. The fundamental clauses of the convention empowered plant-breeders to license nurseries that proposed to propagate the breeders' varieties and allowed a breeder to charge commission on all plants budded and sold. The convention also applied to seeds and other means of growing plants, and commercial seed suppliers, as for grain and cereals, particularly benefited by it. The conditions of the convention were made internationally reciprocal, so that, say, French breeders could have protection for their plants in Germany if German breeders were similarly protected in France, and so forth. In future any propagator of roses had to obtain a licence from the breeder in order to be allowed to multiply and to sell plants of the variety concerned, and he had to pay a commission on each plant raised. There are some minor exceptions, notably in the case of plants not raised for sale. If a town parks department chooses to bud some roses in order to multiply the number in the parks, then there is no commission to be paid. Likewise, an amateur gardener who makes a hobby of raising roses for his own use has nothing to fear from the rights regulations.

In some cases, and particularly with roses, the rights were extended to cover the propagation of plants for the purpose of producing cut-blooms.

For the breeders the new rights were a new beginning and from them arose a stronger and more soundly based industry.

It could not be expected that this new situation in the rose industry was going to be popular with the propagating nurseries, which up to this time had considered it their absolute right to propagate and sell whatever rose they wished. This freedom to pick other people's brains and to usurp their work had always been a sore point with breeders; it was a kind of piracy, there could be no doubt about that, but 'piracy' is not a word one can use freely of an act that the law does not recognize as illegal.

Nowadays, with plant rights legally enforceable, a proportion of the price at which a rose is sold to the public represents a commission paid to the breeder. In Britain at the present time a new variety is marketed in the first year at a price in the region of 60p, and of this amount roughly 12p is the commission. Thereafter, as the rose ceases to be a novelty and the price falls in the fifth year to about 35p, the commission reduces too, to 3p, at which it remains for up to a further ten years.

You, my reader and I hope my customer, may be saying that this is another charge that has to be paid out of the pocket of the public. I suppose that it is, for the money must come from the ultimate purchaser, but I would strongly deny that it has made roses more expensive. It has made the industry more cost conscious. The prices of roses have necessarily risen with the increase of all the costs concerned in producing them, but the rise has been nothing like as steep as in many other products. It is an interesting fact that between the wars my father was selling new roses at five shillings or seven and sixpence each: the equivalents of those prices today would be at least twice the level now common throughout the trade.

The present situation in the United States remains that of

protection by plant patents. The U.S. has not yet signed the rights convention, although a system of rights has recently passed through Congress protecting grain crops. This cannot, I think, go on for long. American breeders would like to do business in Europe on the same footing as Europeans. The Iron Curtain satellites would probably also like to adhere to the convention, and no doubt they will eventually do so, and that will be considerably to our advantage.

The question of control remains to be discussed here. A compulsory licensing clause in the convention stipulates that breeders shall grant licences to anyone who applies, and this for a time they did do, and found themselves giving licences very uneconomically to people who proposed to propagate very small numbers of plants or whose intentions were airy ambitions not likely to be realized. To avoid this kind of thing we now charge a minimum fee of £100 for a licence.

The established nurseries, of course, are in a very different position. They are entitled to licences and we cannot unreasonably refuse them, but there has to be some means of regulating the numbers of plants propagated and sold. At first we did this by insisting on a commission on every plant sold but by this method we, the breeders, were underwriting the risks—if the nursery had a bad year, from poor management or bad salesmanship or any other cause, it was reflected in our returns. So what we do now is to grant a licence to propagate an agreed number of plants. The licensed nursery may then raise plants up to the figure agreed, and whether it sells them all or not is no direct concern of ours.

In some countries there is inspection to ensure that nurseries are not raising more plants than they are licensed to raise. In Holland inspectors are employed by the government to ensure that nurseries are not illegally propagating protected varieties. In Germany Tantau and Kordes have agreed to inspect. In Britain there is no organized inspectorate up to this moment of time; any breeder who wants to make a check must do it for himself. I have some fifty nurseries licensed in these islands, and of course they cannot all be visited frequently, nor is there any such need; but when it is necessary it is no difficult task to estimate how many of one kind of rose may be growing in a field. An experienced man, which any nurseryman should be, can easily estimate how many roses there are in a row and how many rows in a field, and if the estimate does not correspond to the licence then there is reason to take action.

Control is also exercised by the labelling system. I insist that every rose plant should have a label attached bearing the name and the patent number of the rose together with our familiar rose and shamrock mark. If a plant is sold without this label then it is being sold illegally. Some breeders have now extended the labelling system to include cut-roses, and these also must be labelled, but in this case only one in ten roses need carry the label.

All this talk of control and checks suggests that plant-breeders are perpetually at war with propagating nurseries and have good reason to be suspicious of them. In fact, there was quite a bit of opposition to the system in the begining. We had some hot-heads who boycotted our roses because we insisted on their using our labels. Others said the commission rates were too high. Harry Wheatcroft, backed by a number of other propagators, actually took me to the Rights Office to have one of my patents disallowed and won what I might call a technical knock-out.

All these things only made me more determined. Only Meilland and Poulsen really supported me. I dug in my heels, faced the wrath of the trade, and insisted on my labels and commission rates. In the end the opposition collapsed, as it was hurting them not to have my roses. Now that this initial skirmishing is over, breeders and nurserymen have shaken down into a wary but generally cheerful relationship. They are gradually discovering that each depends on the other. A good new rose like Mullard Jubilee or Molly McGredy is good for everybody.

8. GREAT ROSES OF OUR TIME

I suppose that I should begin by defining the qualities of a great rose. That is not an easy thing to do and there may be as many different opinions as there are rose-growers. A great rose must, of course, have attraction for the eye, though not necessarily for the nose—fragrance is not a quality of all roses that are undoubtedly great. It should be novel when it first appears, but novelty alone will not make a rose great. An important factor is colour. Certainly a great rose should have a good shape of bloom, but it should above all have a good colour, something that will make it admired and continue to be admired. If it is red it will already have an advantage because red is always the most popular colour in roses. As for the plant, it must be of good habit and it must have the kind of vigour that can maintain its quality and character through thousands, perhaps millions of propagations over many years. No rose is great if its stock begins to fade after seven or eight years, or if buyers become disenchanted with its performance and sales fall off. There is the fundamental quality of a great rose —its performance in garden or park over decades and in a variety of climates in different countries. To survive it will have to grow well in different soils and different climates and in various weathers, it will have to be disease-resistant or disease-free, and frost-proof if possible, with a strong constitution that quickly recovers from set-backs.

Qualities such as these, with the ability to grow and to flourish without the need for onerous attention, will make a rose loved and kept and will make it talked about, and such talk is better than the best advertisement on paper; but they will not of themselves make it desired and bought. Primarily, it is the beauty of

Picasso

the flower that first attracts attention to a rose, that comes first in conversation, but many roses are beautiful that nevertheless cannot be called great roses. It is what underlies the beauty, the solid basic qualities of ease of maintenance, endurance, tolerance, and so on that keep a rose in being in various countries and throughout a long life.

There are a lot of fine roses of the past that I know nothing about and what follows in this chapter represents for the greater part my own personal preferences or my personal experience.

The first great McGredy rose was Countess of Gosford, which I have never seen; it appears to have been a big, globular, heavily veined pink rose. About that time (1901) Frau Karl Druschki was a real landmark, the first really snow-white rose. Then there were two red Dickson roses, Hugh Dickson and George Dickson, which were hybrid perpetuals, with enormous blowzy blooms with high fragrance, really very good in their day. The Queen Alexandra Rose, bred by my grandfather, was the first bicolour, in red and yellow, the start of all the bicolours. Grandfather bred it from the Austrian Copper, and this is an interesting series to follow through. Queen Alexandra seems now a rather scruffy red and yellow hybrid tea—though Mansfield describes it as 'bright vermilion with reverse of old gold'—but at that time it was considered, and indeed it was, magnificent. It was used as one of the parents of Margaret McGredy, in 1927, the rose named after my grandmother, which for years and years was one of *the* red roses, one of the first with strong vigour—it had the hybrid vigour typical, for example, of the Queen Elizabeth rose. Margaret McGredy is very much in the background of Peace— it is a grandparent of Peace on both sides, a thing that many people find incredible because Peace is a bright yellow rose. Kronenbourg (*facing page* 72) is a sport of Peace, reverting back to the colour of The Queen Alexandra Rose—unexpected, but the kind of thing that can happen in rose-breeding. This sport was found in my fields by two of my staff, who brought it to me. I gave them fifty pounds apiece for their percipience and one of

K

137

them used the money to buy a motor-bike, which was thereafter known as Kronenbourg.

The 1920s and 1930s had a number of roses of interest. There was the dark red Étoile de Hollande, from Verschuren (it actually came in 1919), which was an important red hybrid tea, with a long pointed bud and an ineffable scent. In the 1950s it was still a good rose and I can imagine that in 1919 it must have been stupendous. Nowadays it seems dreadful, hanging its head, sprawly in habit, and prone to disease. Madame Butterfly was popular from the twenties onwards, and people still hark back to it with affection. Bred by Hill in 1918, it had a soft pink flower with a very sweet scent. Shot Silk, from Dickson, was also very fragrant. These three roses are still about, and you might conclude from them that all the best roses of the twenties must have been fragrant. It would not be true. Shot Silk, which came out in 1923, is still, by present-day standards, a pretty rose, and it has now, and only now, begun to fall from popularity.

The year 1924 saw the arrival of Else Poulsen, the first of the true Poulsen polyanthas. Very free-flowering and very frost-hardy, it is still grown all over the world and is seen in large quantities in Denmark and Scandinavia generally and in the U.S.A. It is not fragrant and is rather a harsh pink by present standards.

McGredy's Yellow, 1933, which has died only in the last two or three years, but is still shown in some catalogues, was for long the best yellow. Mrs. Sam McGredy, named after my mother in 1929, is only now beginning to lose its popularity, but it was in its day phenomenal—there has never been a rose of so good a colour, or of such a colour, a kind of coppery scarlet flower in copper-beech foliage. It has been available from us for forty years. The climbing form is still good and is grown extensively. McGredy's Ivory is a rose that needs reasonably good weather, but it was very good in its day. There are white roses now that are more weather-resistant, and it has been replaced in particular by a rose called Pascali.

Crimson Glory, from Kordes in 1935, was the best red for a long time. This and Étoile de Hollande were *the* two red roses of my youth. Crimson Glory had a wonderful fragrance. It is in the background of nearly every good rose of today—of Fashion, for example, which leads on to Spartan and to all the salmons, and it is in the background of all the red hybrid teas.

The Poulsen series, which gave rise to the floribundas, beginning with Else Poulsen, went on to Anne-Mette Poulsen, Karen Poulsen, and Kirsten Poulsen, and then in 1938 Poulsen produced the first of the yellow floribundas, Poulsen's Yellow, a startling rose in its time, though it has been surpassed since. Then there was Poulsen's Copper (1940), which was in colour rather like the Austrian Copper.

Two Dickson roses deserve mention, each the best rose in its colour. Betty Uprichard was a pink bicolour hybrid tea and Barbara Richards a buff hybrid tea. One of ours, Christopher Stone, with extra-big strong foliage, was a very fragrant hybrid tea named for the broadcaster Christopher Stone, who was well known at that time. Hector Deane, named for the surgeon who took out my tonsils, was a fragrant salmon-pink rose that was popular for a long time. Then in 1937, three years after his death, my father's McGredy's Sunset appeared. It was the first of the orange-yellow blends that was frost-hardy. The flower was small, but the colour was a great improvement on anything of the kind that had gone before. This rose has been out of circulation for five or six years, but it can still be found in Scandinavia, where frost-hardiness is important. About the same time Kordes' Orange Triumph—which was not orange but scarlet—was popular; it was a big plant with small, clustered flowers, mildew-resistant, black-spot-resistant, frost-resistant—a very healthy plant still to be seen in lots of gardens.

After the last war Meilland dominated the market with his Peace and his Eden Rose, which are among the greatest, and then with Grand'mère Jenny. Then came the Americans with the rise of the floribunda roses. The U.S.A. did not suffer from the kind of interruption the war caused in Europe, and that helped to put them ahead. Nor, curiously, at least at first, did the Germans— they sold more roses from 1940 to 1942 than ever before. A lot of people buy roses when things are prosperous and they have reason to be cheerful, and the war was going well for Germany until 1942. After that, of course, the German rose business went to pot in tune with the disasters and defeats of the Third Reich.

In America after the war the concentration on the floribunda produced some fine roses, at a time when European nurseries were still recovering from a concentration on onions, tomatoes, and other mundane plants. Gene Boerner's Fashion came in 1947, the first of the good salmon-pink floribundas and a sensation, to be followed the next year by Masquerade, the unique rose that changes colour from yellow to red. Then in 1950 came Kordes' Independence, an orange-scarlet floribunda quite different in the quality of its colour. These were all successful roses, all breaks into new fields, all startling, and they are in the background of nearly all modern hybrids. Independence was the forerunner of all the bright oranges that we have now—it is in the parentage of Super Star, Orangeade, Irish Mist, and others.

In 1948 Spek's Yellow was the first deep yellow with a good plant. Jan Spek did not raise it; he saw it in some garden or other and bought it for a few hundred pounds, and it made tens of thousands of pounds for him; it helped to make his name internationally known. Herb Swim raised Circus, which was also a good yellow, and he also raised Sutter's Gold, in 1950, the first healthy, really fragrant yellow hybrid tea. It had a long bud with a bloom with red in it, and for years it was one of my favourite roses.

Ena Harkness was raised, not by Jack Harkness, but by a man called Norman, a diamond-setter, who was an amateur in rose-breeding, with a back-garden and a tiny greenhouse. For an amateur to raise a good rose in these circumstances is like winning the big prize on the pools. And Norman did it *twice* in quick succession, first with Ena Harkness and then with Frensham, both out in 1946. Both were truly great roses—Frensham was the standard red floribunda for years. Unfortunately for Norman, there was no plant protection at that time and he made little money out of his fine roses.

There was nothing very much after 1950 until in 1954 Spartan rocketed into the sky with the massive advertising campaign of Jackson & Perkins. Spartan is in the background of practically everything I have bred. It is the mother, or the grandmother, or somewhere in the line, of Mischief, of Elizabeth of Glamis, of Violet Carson, of City of Leeds, and others.

Queen Elizabeth came from Lammerts of California in 1955. It is a clear pink rose on a good plant, with hybrid vigour that Lammerts got by bringing together two lines that were far apart. A year later Allgold appeared from the Norfolk breeder Le Grice, a deep yellow rose that was among the best yellow floribundas for a long time; the flower is rather small and the plant is subject to black spot, but it was a definite landmark. It is still being sold and is probably the most popular of the deep-yellow floribundas.

Perfecta, 1957, was one of the first roses Kordes introduced from the parentage of Karl Herbst. (It is of interest that if you took almost any good yellow hybrid tea rose in those days and put Karl Herbst pollen on it, you got a good result. Kordes taught us all this and went on to other things. I did it with McGredy's Yellow and got Piccadilly.) Perfecta was a sensation at the time, a magnificent, big, cream-coloured rose with pink on the edges and a record number of petals (seventy). Kordes followed in 1958 with Iceberg, the best white rose ever bred and still the largest-selling white floribunda. It got a gold medal from the Royal National Rose Society, and that was a remarkable honour for a white rose.

Wendy Cussons was named in 1959 for the wife of the well-known soap manufacturer. A splendid rose in Britain and in many other parts, it is very fragrant, but I do not like the colour, which is too hard for my taste, although it has been called 'sparkling cerise'. It is a very popular rose, and it won the President's Trophy in 1959. It was bred by Gregory, an important nurseryman in Nottingham, and this was his first attempt at hybridizing. It was an astonishing achievement to come up first time with a rose good enough to win the President's Trophy.

1960 was the year of Super Star, raised by Tantau, which I

account one of the greatest roses of my lifetime, and probably the most popular rose grown today, even in this time of Peace. It was a vintage year for me too, with Piccadilly, which is still the biggest-selling bicolour in the world, and Mischief (*facing page* 20) which won the President's Trophy for me that year. Mischief came from a cross of Spartan and Peace—take two of the best roses like those and there is always a likelihood of a good offspring among the seedlings.

The sixties, I am proud to say, were greatly influenced by the roses I bred: Mischief in 1961, Paddy McGredy in 1962, Elizabeth of Glamis in 1964, and a lot more roses like those. Paddy McGredy was the first floribunda rose to have true hybrid tea form in the blooms. From elsewhere came King's Ransom (Morey, 1961), which is still the standard against which yellow hybrid tea roses are judged. De Ruiter of Holland introduced Europeana, which, with Lili Marlene, reigns over the kingdom of red parks roses. Pascali, that same year, was the first white hybrid tea that was really satisfactory, really rain-resistant. From Louis Lens, of Belgium, it is the best of this kind on the market at the moment. Fragrant Cloud, by Tantau, out in 1964, was an obvious winner; a seedling of Super Star, it has many of the qualities of Super Star plus very good foliage and a memorable fragrance— its minus point is that the old flowers go a bad colour.

Papa Meilland, from Meilland of course (1963), mildews too much ever to be really popular, but it bears the most beautiful crimson blooms in the world; in less lush climates, where the plant grows smaller and tougher and resists mildew, it makes a magnificent rose.

My rose Uncle Walter (*facing page* 44) is a mammoth plant, growing to five feet and bearing a deep red bloom, which is outstanding in most moist, cool climates; it was the product of a new way of breeding hybrid teas back through climbers.

In 1964 Tantau's Blue Moon was introduced, not the best blue in my opinion—I prefer Silver Star from Kordes—but the most successful to date.

In 1965 Poulsen introduced Pernille Poulsen, a soft pink, which is one of the earliest roses to come into bloom—it is a good point for a rose if it comes early. The following year brought my City of Leeds (*facing page* 88), which is established as probably the best deep salmon-pink; it won a gold medal and is a very outstanding rose in England. In 1967 Jack Harkness introduced his first rose, Escapade, and it was a good one, the result of imaginative thinking before starting to breed—he took two widely different strains to raise this rose. Free-flowering, and lilac pink, it looks very distinct from any other rose.

In 1966 my rose Jan Spek (*facing page* 84), with a medium-yellow bloom that goes creamy yellow before petal-fall, was the rose of the year and two years later it was awarded the Golden Thorn at Belfast.

Any rose later than 1966 is still too young to have proved itself without doubt one of the company of great roses, but there is no lack of contenders for the distinction. Kordes' Peer Gynt, a hybrid tea, is the deepest yellow rose of the time, and my Irish Mist (*facing page* 104) is the most perfectly formed of the orange-salmon roses. Who is to say whether these two, or Molly McGredy, or City of Belfast (*facing page* 108), are going to be successful enough to join the august company of the great?

Then, too, there are the climbing roses, scarcely considered because climbers have never been among the most popular roses—gardeners will plant a dozen or more floribundas for every climber. Breeders have thought that there was not a market for climbers big enough to deserve much attention. Kordes and I are busy showing the world that there is more in climbers than was supposed.

Kordes began to raise climbers from a species he had called *Rosa Kordesii*, a chance cross from a *rugosa*, one of those occasions when one rare seed among thousands of infertile ones sets and grows. The climbers Kordes developed from this strain will withstand the winter even in the United States. The best-known examples are Hamburger Phoenix, Sympathie, and Leverkusen.

I took Coral Dawn, one of Gene Boerner's roses, and one of Kordes' called Heidelberg, and I crossed these and raised Handel (*see front cover*), Schoolgirl (*facing page* 52), Swan Lake, Bantry Bay, and Galway Bay, and all of these roses are very popular and in the running for the distinction of the adjective 'great'.

Because Kordes and I have a head start in raising new climbers, we have so far had little competition to contend with. In my youth climbers were roses that flowered once in summer, and that was that. Now the new climbers Kordes and I have raised will flower all the summer through and no one else has anything of the kind. In Britain I have my own and I am agent for Kordes' roses too.

9. THE FUTURE

What is going to happen in the seventies? A row of successes for McGredy? I hope, I hope! A blue rose? That I am not prepared to forecast. I think the 'hand-painted' roses that have started with Picasso are going to be important in my breeding programmes for the future. Picasso (*facing page* 136) is so unusual as to be almost bizarre, a bicolour with petals brilliant scarlet and snow-white at the same time. There has certainly been no other rose like this. It has come on the market in 1971, the first of a series of floribundas and hybrid teas. In that series will be colour-combinations of red and white, red and yellow, red and pink, and I don't know what else. I have them in floribundas and in hybrid teas, and I have them, or shall have them, in miniatures, and I shall have them in climbers—in fact, I intend to have them in just about every form.

In my opinion breeders in the seventies are going to be a lot more selective concerning what they put on the market. Bronze-yellow, deep, deep, bronzy yellow, the copper kind of colour, is going to become available on plants much more healthy than now. At the moment there is a series of roses, including Vienna Charm, Old Timer, Whisky Mac, that are very popular roses in that colour, but these plants are all frost-prone and subject to disease. We are just on the verge of a breakthrough to a better colour and to more satisfactory plants. Today it is just as it was with yellow in the forties and fifties, when yellow was not available on a fully durable plant. Allgold was the first yellow to be at all satisfactory, and it is only since the advent of Arthur Bell (*facing page* 76) and Jan Spek (*facing page* 84) and Chinatown, and some of the other, newer yellow floribundas that we have had plants that are absolutely winter-hardy so that frost will not kill them. Among hardy hybrid teas we now have Peer Gynt and Grandpa Dickson. Formerly, if you planted a bed of yellow hybrid teas you lost some of them every year by frost. Well, we are at a similar stage today with the copper colours.

Seán Jennett would be interested in thornless roses—he has one growing as a chance seedling in his garden. There have been a few thornless roses from as far back as 1873, when Zéphirine Drouhin appeared, but there seems to be no general demand for them. On the contrary, some roses are admired just for the sake of their thorns, big yellow or red thorns that are a feature of the plant. A rose species called *Rosa omeiensis pteracantha* has huge red thorns aligned along the stem, and these thorns are translucent and magnificent when seen with the light shining through them. I do not think that this rose would be grown if it were not for its thorns, though its hips, orange-red and pear-shaped, are also attractive. Thorns and hips carry the charm of such a rose over a long period beyond the time of blooming. If all roses were to be bred without thorns we would have to amend a lot of the world's poetry!

Plant qualities are going to be important in the future. We tend to look on roses at present as something to fill a bed with colour for a few months of the year, but I think that roses, or some roses, are going to become garden plants of beauty whether the blooms are on them or not. They will be prized for the colour of the foliage, for example. There are roses with attractive foliage even now—Brasilia is an instance, with fine, fat, blood-red foliage that turns a coppery-green. Well, there are going to be more in that field.

Then there is fragrant foliage—odorous foliage is nothing new, for there is a species that has leaves with a powerful, magnificent scent, not a scent of roses, but a scent with a minty flavour. There is no reason why foliage fragrance should not be bred through to modern roses, so that the rose-bed will be full of scent even when there is no bloom on the plants. I am working along this line, though not yet with the results I want—but it will come, someone will get there.

Next, the grace of growth of the plant is going to be more important than it has been. Look at Peace; it is a very beautiful, very healthy rose, and immensely popular, but it is a large and gawky plant. Form is going to receive more attention. One expects a rose at present to grow straight up, though not to grow too tall—it goes to three feet and then flowers on top. Why should we not have roses that will grow three feet tall and then arch their stems over and down to the ground again in graceful curves all round from the centre, with flowers all along the stems? There is a little gem of a pink rose from Japan, called Nozomi, that will do exactly that. It has a fault, that it flowers once only, though for a good period. Nurserymen in Britain are just beginning to take it up—though it is our business always to produce new things, it is surprising how conservative we rose-breeders really are. But Gregory has it in his catalogue already. There is another rose with a similar habit, called Sea Foam, but it is more profuse and vigorous and will probably make a great mound, four or five feet tall.

Another line along which I have been working is the rose planted for ground-cover. I have one called Sunday Times. You could not imagine how thorny it is! It grows low and mats together into a solid prickly mass that will deter any dog. It gets so thick eventually that weeds have trouble to thrive beneath it, and so it maintains itself clean and clear.

There are other possibilities, endless possibilities, but I do not think that I am going to start anything completely new now, to begin from scratch to produce something that does not yet exist. I am thirty-nine and it might be fifteen or twenty years, or longer, if I begin now, before anything came from that new line; so I shall keep to things the useful fruition of which I am likely to see in my working life. I shall be lucky if I see the full development of the ground-cover line, though I am ten years ahead and Sunday Times is on sale in 1971. There must come a time when I shall prefer to potter, to be a dilettante. Running a successful, large-scale rose-breeding organization needs a lot of money, a lot of capital, and to be viable it has to be linked with a big commercial propagating and marketing department. It would be delightful if there were some efficient person to run the commercial side so that from now on I could concentrate on breeding roses. As it is I have to be a salesman as well as a rose-breeder. If I am to escape ulcers, high blood-pressure, and the other diseases of business-men, I cannot go on for a lot longer leading the kind of life I have led these last twenty years. I have spent I do not know how many hours racing about in aeroplanes, travelled I do not know how many thousands of air-miles, lived an unconscionable part of my life in hotels, and I have seen too little of my wife and my two children. I grow old—not yet, praise God, but none of us can escape at last, and one day there must come an end to the frenzy of this life of roses.

APPENDIXES

APPENDIX 1

THE McGREDY FAMILY OF ROSES

Since the foundation of the nursery the family has raised over 265 new varieties, all of which have been on the market. The following short list is made up of McGredy roses that have been very popular over a large part of the world or that have been remarkable in breeding.

1906 COUNTESS OF GOSFORD
Salmon-pink hybrid tea.
Gold Medal, R.N.R.S.

1908 HIS MAJESTY
Fragrant, dark-crimson hybrid tea.
Gold Medal, R.N.R.S.

1909 LADY ALICE STANLEY
Bright-pink hybrid tea.
Gold Medal, R.N.R.S.

1910 MRS. HERBERT STEVENS
White hybrid tea.
Gold Medal, R.N.R.S.

1912 BRITISH QUEEN
Fragrant white hybrid tea.
Gold Medal, R.N.R.S.

1913 OLD GOLD
Deep-gold hybrid tea.
Gold Medal, R.N.R.S.

1916 ISOBEL
Single, light rose-pink hybrid tea.
Gold Medal, R.N.R.S.

1917 GOLDEN EMBLEM
Madame Melanie Soupert × Constance
Fragrant canary yellow hybrid tea.
Gold Medal, R.N.R.S.

1918 CHRISTINE
Deep golden-yellow hybrid tea.
Gold Medal, R.N.R.S.

EMMA WRIGHT
Orange-shaded salmon hybrid tea. A unique colour in its day.

THE QUEEN ALEXANDRA ROSE
Fragrant, bright-red, reverse-shaded old-gold hybrid tea. One of the parents of Margaret McGredy, which in its turn was a parent of Peace. The sport of Peace, Kronenbourg, reverts to the colour of The Queen Alexandra Rose.
Gold Medal, R.N.R.S.

1919 MRS. HENRY MORSE
Cream-tinted, flesh-coloured rose marked and veined red; hybrid tea. Fragrant.
Gold Medal, R.N.R.S.

1920 MRS. CHARLES LAMPLOUGH
Enormous white hybrid tea; it was in the background of many of the early McGredy roses, notably McGredy's Yellow.
Gold Medal, R.N.R.S.

1926 MRS. A. R. BARRACLOUGH
Very bright carmine-pink hybrid tea.
Gold Medal, R.N.R.S.

1927 MARGARET McGREDY
Named for my grandmother. In its day, a magnificently
vigorous healthy hybrid tea of bright orange-scarlet. A
very important parent.
Gold Medal, R.N.R.S.

1929 MRS. SAM McGREDY
(*Donald Macdonald × Golden Emblem*) × (*Seedling × The
Queen Alexandra Rose*)
Named for my mother. Probably our most famous rose,
producing hybrid-tea blooms of scarlet-copper-orange,
with glossy, reddish-bronze foliage. Infuriatingly, it was
an indifferent breeder.
Gold Medal, R.N.R.S.

McGREDY'S IVORY
Mrs. Charles Lamplough × Mabel Morse
Very big ivory white hybrid tea of perfect form.
Gold Medal, R.N.R.S.

1931 PORTADOWN FRAGRANCE
An extremely fragrant pink hybrid tea.
Gold Medal, R.N.R.S.

1932 PICTURE
Small, clear rose-pink hybrid tea. Never received any
great honour, although it has been one of our most
successful roses.

1933 SOUTHPORT
(*Souvenir de George Dickson × Crimson Queen*) × *George
Beckwith*
Very fragrant, long pointed bud, bright-red hybrid tea.
Gold Medal, R.N.R.S.

McGREDY'S YELLOW

Mrs. Charles Lamplough × (*The Queen Alexandra Rose* × *J. B. Clark*)
A very outstanding bright buttercup-yellow hybrid tea. Absolutely perfect form.
Gold Medal, R.N.R.S.

1937 McGREDY'S SUNSET

Margaret McGredy × *Mabel Morse*
A pretty tone of chrome yellow shaded light scarlet; extremely hardy in its day for this kind of hybrid-tea colour.

REX ANDERSON

Florence L. Izzard × *Mrs. Charles Lamplough*
An enormous white hybrid tea which did particularly well in the U.S.A.

SAM McGREDY

Delightful × *Mrs. Charles Lamplough*
For my money, an absolute dud, which should never have been given that name. It just wouldn't grow, producing normally one big shoot with one or two absolutely perfect hybrid-tea blooms on top. Light buff.
Gold Medal, R.N.R.S.

1938 HECTOR DEANE

McGredy's Scarlet × *Lesley Dudley*
A very fragrant, orange-carmine and pink hybrid tea. The man took out my tonsils!
Clay Cup for Fragrance, R.N.R.S.

1946 CYNTHIA BROOKE

Le Progrès × (*Madame Melanie Soupert* × *Le Progrès*)
An unusually deep ochre-yellow hybrid tea. Completely unfading.

154

1948 RUBAIYAT
(*McGredy's Scarlet* × *Mrs. Sam McGredy*) × (*Seedling* × *Sir Basil McFarland*)
Very fragrant, deep rose-red hybrid tea.
Winner of the All-America Award in 1947

1949 GREY PEARL
(*Mrs. Charles Lamplough* × *Seedling*) × (*Sir David Davis* × *Southport*)
Lavender-grey, shaded olive and tan, hybrid tea. To most people, a revolting colour, but a forerunner of many of today's lavender blues.

1959 ORANGEADE
Orange Sweetheart × *Independence*
Single bright-orange floribunda.
Gold Medals: R.N.R.S., Hamburg, and Portland, Oregon
Herr Mock Medal for the Best Rose of the Floriade, Rotterdam

1960 PICCADILLY
McGredy's Yellow × *Karl Herbst*
One of today's most popular hybrid tea roses. Red and yellow bicolour.
Gold Medals: Madrid, Rome, and Rotterdam
Nord-Rose Award Winner for Scandinavia

1961 MISCHIEF
Peace × *Spartan*
Small-flowered salmon hybrid tea (*facing page 20*).
Gold Medal and the President's International Trophy 1961, R.N.R.S.
Gold Medals: Hamburg, and Portland, Oregon
Nord-Rose Award Winner, Scandinavia

DAILY SKETCH
Ma Perkins × *Grand Gala*
Very fragrant pink and silver bicolour floribunda.
Gold Medal, R.N.R.S.

1962 EVELYN FISON (Irish Wonder)
Moulin Rouge × *Korona*
Fragrant scarlet floribunda (*facing page 24*).
Gold Medal, R.N.R.S.

PADDY McGREDY
Spartan × *Tzigane*
Very well formed, deep rose-pink floribunda.
Gold Medal, R.N.R.S.
Nord-Rose Award Winner, Scandinavia

1963 UNCLE WALTER
Brilliant × *Heidelberg*
High-centred, crimson-scarlet hybrid tea (*facing page 44*).
Nord-Rose Award Winner, Scandinavia
Gold Medal, Copenhagen

VIOLET CARSON
Madame Léon Cuny × *Spartan*
Well formed, light-salmon floribunda with silvery reverse.
Violet Carson plays the meddling Ena Sharples in *Coronation Street*.

CASINO (Gerbe d'Or)
Coral Dawn × *Buccaneer*
Fragrant, soft-yellow climber (*facing page 40*).
Gold Medal, R.N.R.S.

1964 JOHN CHURCH
Ma Perkins × *Red Favourite*
Well formed orange-scarlet floribunda and one of our most popular roses at the present time.

ELIZABETH OF GLAMIS (Irish Charm)
Spartan × *Highlight*
Very fragrant salmon-pink floribunda, named after Her Majesty the Queen Mother (*facing page 56*).
Gold Medal and the President's International Trophy 1963, R.N.R.S.

ELIZABETH OF GLAMIS (Irish Charm) (*cont.*)
Nord-Rose Award Winner, Scandinavia
Gold Medal, Copenhagen
Clay Cup for Fragrance, R.N.R.S.

1965 KRONENBOURG (Flaming Peace)
A sport of Peace. At its best, brilliant scarlet hybrid tea with silvery yellow reverse. The colour fades quickly to a deep rosy purple that either appeals or causes anger (*facing page* 72).

ARTHUR BELL
Clare Grammerstorf × Piccadilly
A very fragrant deep-yellow floribunda paling to creamy yellow. Extremely healthy and winter-hardy (*facing page* 76).
Uladh Award, Rose Society of Northern Ireland

HANDEL
Heidelberg × Columbine
A most unusual climber with cream flowers edged deep rose-pink. One of my most successful roses.
Prize of the Dutch Nurserymen's Association, The Hague

SHANNON
Queen Elizabeth × McGredy's Yellow
Bright, even-pink hybrid tea.
All-German Rose Selection

1966 LADY SETON
Ma Perkins × Mischief
Very fragrant light-pink hybrid tea.
Clay Cup for Fragrance, R.N.R.S.

JAN SPEK
Clare Grammerstorf × Faust
Very winter-hardy light-yellow floribunda (*facing page* 84).
Golden Rose of The Hague
Golden Thorn of the Rose Society of Northern Ireland

CITY OF LEEDS
Evelyn Fison × (*Spartan* × *Red Favourite*)
Even-salmon floribunda (*facing page* 88).
Gold Medal, R.N.R.S.

GALWAY BAY
Heidelberg × *Queen Elizabeth*
Salmon-pink climber.

ICE WHITE (Vision Blanc)
Madame Léon Cuny × (*Orange Sweetheart* × *Independence*)
Snowy white floribunda.
Gold Medal, Italian Rose Society

1967 IRISH MIST
Orangeade × *Mischief*
Very well formed orange-salmon floribunda (*facing page* 104).

BANTRY BAY
New Dawn × *Korona*
Very free-flowering pink climber.

1968 TIMOTHY EATON
Radar × *Mischief*
Very fragrant salmon hybrid tea.

CITY OF BELFAST
Evelyn Fison × (*Circus* × *Korona*)
Flaming orange floribunda (*facing page* 108).
Gold Medal and President's International Trophy, R.N.R.S.
Gold Medals: Geneva and New Zealand
Golden Thorn of the Rose Society of Northern Ireland
Nord-Rose Award Winner, Scandinavia

1969 SILENT NIGHT
Daily Sketch × *Hassan*
Light yellow hybrid tea.
Gold Medal, Geneva

MOLLY McGREDY
Paddy McGredy × (*Madame Léon Cuny* × *Columbine*)
Rose red and silver bicolour floribunda.
Gold Medal and President's International Trophy, 1968, R.N.R.S.

PANIA
Paddy McGredy × (*Perfecta* × *Montezuma*)
Well formed light-pink hybrid tea.
Gold Medal, New Zealand International Trials

GINGER ROGERS
Super Star × *Miss Ireland*
Light salmon-orange hybrid tea.
Medal of the Belgian Rose Society for Fragrance

1970 COURVOISIER
Elizabeth of Glamis × *Casanova*
Very fragrant bronze-yellow floribunda.

MULLARD JUBILEE (Electron)
Paddy McGredy × *Prima Ballerina*
Very fragrant, deep rose-pink hybrid tea (*facing page 120*).
Gold Medals: R.N.R.S., The Hague, and Baden-Baden
Nord-Rose Award, Scandinavia

NATIONAL TRUST
Evelyn Fison × *King of Hearts*
Very free-flowering, well formed, red hybrid tea.

SATCHMO
Evelyn Fison × *Diamant*
Flaming scarlet floribunda (*facing page 116*).
Gold Medals: The Hague and Roeulx

1971 PICASSO
Marlena × [*Evelyn Fison* × (*Orange Sweetheart* × *Frühlingsmorgen*)]
A complete colour-break of red and silver in bizarre markings. Floribunda (*facing page 136*).

APPENDIX 2

THE PRESIDENT'S INTERNATIONAL TROPHY

The President's International Trophy of the Royal National Rose Society is awarded irrespective of class for the best new seedling of the year. The seedling is selected from one of the gold-medal winners. If no seedling is considered good enough in any year the award is not made. The list below gives the names of the roses that have won the trophy since its inception in 1952, together with the names of the breeders.

1952 Moulin Rouge, *fl.*, Meilland.
1953 Concerto, *fl.*, Meilland
1954 Spartan, *fl.*, Boerner
1955 Queen Elizabeth, *fl.-h.t.*, Lammerts
1956 Faust, *fl.*, Kordes
1957 Perfecta, *h.t.*, Kordes
1958 Dickson's Flame, *fl.*, Alec Dickson
1959 Wendy Cussons, *h.t.*, Gregory
1960 Super Star, *h.t.*, Tantau
1961 Mischief, *h.t.*, McGredy
1962 No award
1963 Elizabeth of Glamis, *fl.*, McGredy
1964 Fragrant Cloud, *h.t.*, Tantau
1965 Grandpa Dickson, *h.t.*, Pat Dickson
1966 No award
1967 City of Belfast, *fl.*, McGredy
1968 Molly McGredy, *fl.-h.t.*, McGredy
1969 Red Planet, *h.t.*, Pat Dickson
1970 Alec's Red, *h.t.*, Cocker

INDEX

In this Index all names of roses (species or cultivated) are printed in italics.